Competing Convictions

College of Ripon & York St. John

3 8025 00408559 6

D1584701

COMPETING CONVICTIONS

Robin Gill

SCM PRESS

COLLEGE OF RIPON
AND YORK ST JOHN
LIBRARY

All rights reserved. No part of this publication
may be reproduced, stored in a retrieval system,
or transmitted, in any form or by any means,
electronic, mechanical, photocopying, recording
or otherwise, without the prior permission of the
publisher, SCM Press Ltd.

Copyright © Robin Gill 1989

British Library Cataloguing in Publication Data

Gill, Robin
Competing convictions.
1.   Religion – Sociological perspectives
I. Title.
306′.6

ISBN 0–334–01908–7

First published 1989
by SCM Press Ltd
26–30 Tottenham Road London N1 4BZ

Photoset at The Spartan Press, Lymington, Hants
and printed in Great Britain by
The Camelot Press Ltd
Southampton

To
WILLIAM LEECH
North East Builder and Christian Philanthropist
with much gratitude

Contents

Preface

Some of my ruder, but previously reliable, friends have assured me that I should have completed my current research before writing *Beyond Decline*. I deny this . . . of course. But I cannot deny what an awesome responsibility it is to be given the opportunity mid-career to do five years uninterrupted research without any teaching responsibilities. This research has been motivated by the many encouraging responses, as well as some understandable misgivings, to *Beyond Decline*, but it has been made possible only by the extraordinary generosity of William Leech and the five church charities that he has endowed. As a very inadequate way of thanking him and them I would like to dedicate this book to him.

Competing Convictions is offered as a first-fruit of this research. The middle empirical section attempts to map rural church decline. Next I must try to do the same for urban church decline, before testing some of the strategies that churches might adopt to counter decline. The final section is more theological. It sketches an understanding of theology as a social system. This, too, I hope will form an essential part of my future research. Between the two I should be kept quite busy.

I undertook the necessary research on fundamentalism for chapter 2 at Dartmouth College, New Hampshire, in the summer of 1988, just before starting at Newcastle University. The issue of fundamentalism was already topical in the States as a result of responses to the film *The Last Temptation of Christ*. But on my return to Britain it was *The Satanic Verses*, followed by the excommunication of the Lord Chancellor by the Free Presbyterian Church of Scotland for attending two Catholic funerals, that made it newsworthy. Sadly, very little of the public commentary in either country showed much understanding of the nature of religious fundamentalism. Colleagues in both universities were very helpful in their criticisms and suggestions, especially Gene Garthwaite, Professor of Persian History at Dartmouth. Chapter 3 was prepared on the prompting of Professor Nicholas Lash and Dr Chris

Rowland of Cambridge University and was first delivered there. Chapter 4 is based upon my inaugural lecture at Newcastle (having been carefully tested first on my colleagues at Edinburgh University!) and the following two chapters have both been tested on colleagues there and on Dr Callum Brown of Strathclyde University. Professor Barry Wetherill of Newcastle very kindly checked my statistics to make sure I was committing no howlers. Members of the British Sociological Association's Study Group on Religion, and particularly Graham Howes, also offered several useful observations. The final chapter was first delivered at the Blackfriars Oxford Symposium on Theology and Sociology and an earlier version of it appeared in *Scottish Journal of Theology*. I am most grateful for all of this. Research could soon become a lonely business without the help of good colleagues.

I am certainly lucky to have been given the chance to do this research. But I am even more lucky to have a family which puts up with it. They have become quite expert at explaining my theories on church decline to bemused strangers (usually in response to the tricky question 'What does your father/husband actually *do* with his time?'). So finally to them my love.

1 · Relative Convictions

Sociology, especially when applied to cognitive disciplines, is methodologically inclined towards relativism. Its habitual tendency is to relativize the ideas and cognitive worlds that it seeks to understand. In exploring relationships between ideas and changing social structures and in uncovering the various ways that ideas are relative to these structures, sociological method persistently seems to threaten the very basis of knowledge and rationality. It threatens this basis by treating all ideas as culturally specific and thus as culturally relative. Even scientific knowledge is threatened in this way, since it is manifestly controlled by élite, highly socialized communities, which generate culturally specific conventions and 'orthodoxies' that, over time, can be seen to change radically as society at large changes.

The relativist tendency of sociology *is* methodological. Once it assumes ontological, or perhaps more aptly 'credal', status it is easily dismissed. Any sociological claim to the effect that all ideas are socially relative faces obvious problems of coherence. Presumably such a claim is itself subject to social relativism, change and possible revision. Very quickly an endless chain of sociological enquiry ensues; a sociology of sociological claims about social relativism is soon followed by a sociology of that sociology, and so *ad infinitum*. In retrospect it was a comparatively easy task for Berger to suggest a programme for 'relativizing the relativizers'.[1] Once social relativism assumes ontological status it at once becomes vulnerable to such a programme and soon leads to intellectual absurdity.

Methodological social relativism is not so vulnerable. It is an instrument of enquiry rather than a credal frame. It results from the obvious point that it is not for the sociologist *qua* sociologist to decide which ideas or forms of knowledge are to be excluded from sociological enquiry. The skill of sociologists in cognitive areas is their ability to suggest possible relationships between ideas and social structures. Others (politicians, ecclesiastics, etc.) may feel threatened by this skill and may seek to confine it to some areas and to protect other areas as inviolate. However, such attempts at control clearly do not belong properly to sociological enquiry itself. The latter knows no bounds and when left unfettered innocently threatens all ideas and forms of knowledge, including its own. It even provides those non-sociologists seeking to control it with some of their strongest ammunition both to undermine its procedures and to exploit these procedures to exercise this control. Unconstrained sociological enquiry does not need to claim that all ideas *are* socially relative, it merely treats all ideas *as if they are* socially relative. It does this because very properly it does not discriminate between ideas, treating some as socially relative and others not. Its task is to treat all ideas as socially relative. Hence the threat that it presents to all cognitive disciplines.

It is hardly surprising that a method which treats all ideas as if they are socially relative is easily confused with ontological relativism. Later chapters will note that sociologists themselves sometimes become imperialistic and contribute to this confusion. Further a method is usually adopted not simply because it is a useful heuristic device but because it is also thought to have some correspondence with the external reality that is its object. So, scientists study the physical world as if it has an ordered construction, that is as if it is governed by discernible laws. This is clearly a method. Yet since they believe that they are making 'discoveries' and not simply imposing their ordered projections upon a chaotic universe, the method also signals a belief. At least some order is usually presupposed in the very activity of scientists themselves. Similarly, sociologists treat ideas as socially relative because at least part of the time they believe that they really are socially relative. Without falling into the trap of thoroughgoing ontological relativism, some degree of relativism is usually presumed about social realities.

This presumption is fostered by the very process of observing how ideas are constructed, propagated and controlled by élite groups. The sociology of knowledge encourages its students to observe cognitive disciplines as socially relative processes. In contrast to those fully engaged in a particular cognitive discipline, the sociology of knowledge encourages detachment and comparison. It soon becomes clear that exponents of cognitive disciplines typically create, and then protect, canons. A number of key founding 'fathers' are identified and a body of literature is 'canonized' in order to distinguish one cognitive discipline from another. This literature is then used to control the discipline and to criticize rival versions. It is used to identify academic expertise/excellence/ 'orthodoxy' for 'disciples' and conversely to disparage others. 'Novices' entering a 'discipline' must quickly be disabused of their prior ideas related to the discipline. Works that have been read previously and which do not form part of the 'canon' are dismissed and ridiculed (often without argument) by the 'master'. A new 'rule', usually in the form of an authoritative book-list, tells the 'novices' how they should behave academically in the future and they are enjoined to 'devote ' their time to it.

As will be seen later, the religious terms here are no accident. Academic socialization has much in common with more ancient forms of religious socialization. In a religious system the virtuosi are typically the theologians, monastics or contemplatives. It is their role to refine, protect and preserve sacred knowledge. Apostolicity, canonical status and credal frames become vital in this process. Just as the religious virtuosi are concerned with refining, protecting and preserving 'knowledge', so secular academics too become engaged in these tasks. In observing this across cultures and across disciplines which would normally be regarded as independent from each other, the sociology of knowledge understandably tends to foster relativism.

This process is increasingly observed in many disciplines. If once, for example, it might have been presumed that a course in English literature simply involved the study of what was universally recognized by the educated as classic works of literature, today this is decreasingly the case. There is a growing awareness that 'classic works of literature' are defined by changing élites. In the recent past the judgment of the British intelligentsia was widely accepted by others seeking such a definition. Today other parts of the English-speaking world are breaking away from this cultural hegemony. The list of 'classic works' appears differently in North America, Australia or English-speaking parts of India or Africa. An awareness of these differences soon relativizes assumptions about the appropriateness of any list of 'classic works'.

Again, it is still easy for Western academics to assume that philosophy is properly speaking Western, and in fact largely European, philosophy. To study philosophy means to study a number of key Enlightenment (another term with theological roots) thinkers, such as Hume and Kant, and the traditions that have spawned from them. At the beginning of the century much greater emphasis would have been given to classical thinkers, notably Aristotle and Plato. Few, however, would place Indian thinkers at the centre of their studies. It has readily been assumed that the history of philosophy is the history of Western philosophy. Or, more accurately, it has been assumed that the history of philosophy is the history of the ideas of a small group of thinkers who have come to be identified as philosophers. On this assumption, not everyone who thinks is a philosopher: not even everyone who thinks deeply about the sort of things that philosophers tend to think about is a philosopher. Rather philosophers are those on the accepted philosophy reading-list. Ironically philosophers, who are usually so insistent upon disciplines carefully defining the terms that they use, have failed to agree upon any definition of philosophy itself. In such a situation the reading-list becomes the determinant of what constitutes the discipline.

Sociologists themselves are also manifestly part of the same process. Founding fathers – Comte, Spencer, Marx, Durkheim, Weber, etc. – are identified and individual reading lists determine how the discipline is to be understood by particular sociologists and their disciples. Since all 'novices' already have many assumptions about society long before they become sociologists, they must be quickly disabused and initiated into the 'orthodox' literature. Much that passes for 'sociology' amongst the uninitiated must be dismissed and paths must be cut even through literature that other sociologists claim to be properly sociological. The divisions between Marxist and non-Marxist understandings of sociology must be negotiated. To the theologian they strongly resemble some of the differences between evangelicals and non-evangelicals and cause as much friction in sociology departments as the latter do in theology departments. Deep ideological and moral differences co-exist uneasily within both disciplines. Particular sociologists or theologians are forced to make choices and then, having made their choices, they reinforce these choices through the literature they 'recommend' to others.

The process of establishing a discipline through a literature that is sanctified or canonized leads to some curious results. Amongst these is the practice of continuing to regard a work as seminal long after its methods and contents are discredited. To the outsider it must seem curious that so many methodological disciplines spend so much of their time discussing works whose deficiencies have been so well established over generations. Those defending this practice might argue that students can be taught more effectively in this manner – since they can read the seminal works for themselves and then learn the art of critical scholarship through reading well-honed criticisms. Up to a point this may well be the case. Yet it does not altogether accord with what actually takes place. If it were simply academics teaching students in this way it would accord. Yet it is not. Academics themselves across methodological disciplines spend a disproportionate amount of their time arguing with one another about the works that are regarded as seminal in their discipline and covering and recovering criticisms that have been made for generations. Again this is an activity that has much in common with the function of religious virtuosi refining, protecting and preserving sacred knowledge.

Amongst sociologists this practice is evident amongst both Marxists and non-Marxists. It is of course immediately evident amongst the former. Enormous trouble is taken to present 'authentic' texts of Marx and then to exegete and interpret them. The sociologically naive, like the naive biblical user, will quote Marx out of context and will generalize about 'Marxism', producing in effect harmonies of disparate tenets. The sophisticated sociologist using Marx, like the redaction biblical critic, will be careful to use specific works of Marx or specific redactions within those works, and distinguish their tenets from those of other works. For the sophisticated Marxist sociologist, just as for the sophisticated biblical theologian, hermeneutics and contextual analysis are prerequisites. Only so can the 'sacred' text be refined and made adequately available to the 'faithful' today (whether or not the faithful themselves are fully appreciative of, or even aware of, this complex and painstaking work).

But the practice is also evident amongst non-Marxist sociologists. It is instructive, for example, to note how much time and trouble is spent analysing and re-analysing a work such as Emile Durkheim's *The Elementary Forms of the Religious Life*. Modern scholarship has revealed just how many of the criticisms that are now made of this work were first made in the decade of its initial appearance.[2] Yet the criticisms are still made and re-made from one account of the sociology of religion to another. Most would agree that Durkheim's method was fundamentally flawed in its secondary use of evidence about the Arunta (which was inaccurate), in its evolutionary assumptions about 'primitive' religion, in its understanding of totemism, and in the tautological nature of its functionalist treatment of the relation between religion and society. Despite this widespread agreement the work is still treated as seminal and its thesis is still vigorously debated. However, once it is realized that the work itself has a canonical function in some approaches to sociology, none of this appears so surprising. It is not simply a way of teaching sociological error, it is itself a 'sacred' text.

One of the features of sacred texts is that frequently they can be appropriated by competing groups and communities. The scriptures of long surviving religious traditions are usually sufficiently opaque and pluralistic to allow mutually exclusive interpretations and to nurture competing and sometimes mutually hostile communities. Chapter 7 will explore this phenomenon through recent sociological accounts of earliest Christianity and of biblical interpretation within differing social contexts. A similar analysis could be made of Hindu or Islamic scriptures. In all of these instances, the scriptures themselves are pluralistic and their reception and interpretation through the ages is even more pluralistic. As a result, mutually hostile groups can claim them as their own and anathematize the divergent uses of them by others.

This too can be observed in a number of cognitive disciplines. Durkheim's work is, after all, claimed differently by both sociologists and social anthropologists. In a modern academic world of carefully compartmentalized disciplines, recent works may be less likely to be variously appropriated (although concepts such as 'functionalism' or 'structuralism' clearly cross disciplines). However, founding 'fathers' are in greater demand and are less readily available. Sometimes competing appropriations are largely unknown to modern exponents of the separate disciplines. So both sociologists and theologians have used the writings of Ernst Troeltsch and Richard Niebuhr with little awareness of their separate discussions.[3]

By calling attention to this separate and competing appropriation of founding 'fathers' by different disciplines, a sociology of knowledge again tends to foster relativism. Observing this process, by which academic disciplines attempt to establish credibility and to define and then defend boundaries, contributes to this relativism. By noting its similarities to more ancient forms of religious socialization, it raises suspicions that the procedures of disciplines are not as pragmatic as some of their exponents might wish. In effect, it tends to undermine some confidence in the rationality of cognitive disciplines and of the claims that they make. Thus a suspicion of the social relativism of ideas emerges from the very procedures of a sociology of knowledge. In examining 'knowledge' as manufactured and controlled, it threatens in the process the basis of all knowledge, including ironically its own. Without engaging in imperialistic ontological claims, it nonetheless encourages a form of study which is thoroughly iconoclastic. It seems to be methodologically programmed towards total and, in the end, totally incoherent relativism.

Theology too, once subjected to the scrutiny of the sociology of knowledge, feels the winds of relativism. Theologians may initially derive some satisfaction from the discomfiture of other cognitive disciplines from this scrutiny, especially of those disciplines which have sometimes been hostile to theology. But the satisfaction is only short lived. Having observed that other disciplines use processes analogous to religious socialization, theologians soon realize that such observation also tends to relativize their own discipline. Theology is as pluralistic as philosophy or sociology and theologians adopt procedures comparable to philosophers and sociologists to cope with this pluralism. The founding 'fathers' adopted by one set of theologians are not identical with those of another, and, even when they are, their appropriations differ radically. Theologians use reading-lists to control students and are just as dismissive as their secular counterparts of 'unauthorized' literature. They are just as repetitious as others in their use and re-use of seminal works and just as changeable in their convictions. Once the process of doing theology (as distinct from the contents of theology) becomes an object of sociological scrutiny, relativism seems to be inescapable.

And theology is increasingly an object of sociological scrutiny. More accurately, sociological methods are increasingly being deployed in various branches of academic theology. If once the bias of many theologians was towards classics or philosophy, today sociology is playing an ever more central role within theological studies. Nowhere is this more evident than within New Testament studies.[4] Over the last fifteen years there has been a dramatic growth of New Testament sociology which shows no signs of abating. Approaching New Testament evidence with sociological, rather than just historical or theological, questions has opened the discipline to a new generation of scholars. Not surprisingly it has also heightened a sense of relativism which is seldom entirely absent for the Christian from critical New Testament scholarship. Christian convictions, or the biblical foundations of these convictions, are confronted with what seem to be the corrosive effects of relativism. New Testament sociology appears to be even more corrosive than other methods within the discipline.

In studying competing convictions in recent sectarianism and in Victorian inter-church rivalry, and relative convictions in modern theology, this book will seek to trace various ways in which sociology fosters a sense of relativism. A sociological analysis of those religious groups with the strongest convictions – most evident in the recent resurgence of fundamentalism – heightens this sense of relativism. This resurgence presents a challenge to recent socio-logical models of secularization. In the next chapter I will look for more satisfactory sociological forms of analysis before raising the specifically theological questions that arise from viewing fundamen-talist convictions sociologically. In the third chapter I will examine critically the theory of cognitive dissonance as it seeks to explain the predictions of sectarian groups. The theory is particularly challeng-ing for theology because of its possible extension into New Testament studies. Although I will finally be critical of the basis on which the theory was established (thus making it less applicable to New Testament studies), it does serve to highlight the way the social sciences might clarify and appear to challenge religious convictions.

For the critical theologian the religious subjects of these two chapters will appear somewhat crude. Understanding modern religious fundamentalism is important, but it may not finally challenge a more sophisticated and critical approach to theology. Theologians may feel happy to relativize these particular forms of religious conviction. However, the next four chapters may appear distinctly more corrosive. Whilst many may be happy to use sociology to account for practices and ideas which they regard as frankly erroneous, they may be less happy to apply sociology to their own foundations.

It is commonly held that competing convictions amongst the Victorian churches contributed to their strength, whereas in a more ecumenical age churches compromise on doctrinal issues, are less convinced and indeed convincing to others, and decline accord-ingly. Church decline is regarded as both a product of secularization and an instrument of further secularization. In contrast, it is only conservative, fundamentalist religious movements, mutually com-peting from absolutist tenets, that can hope to thrive in a secular age.

The evidence presented at length in the three middle chapters of this book calls all of this into question. It suggests, quite oppositely, that competing convictions in the context of rural depopulation were instrumental in church decline. Competing convictions which may have been responsible for the rise in churchgoing in the first half of the nineteenth century resulted in decline in the second. I will argue that demography is actually more significant than some supposed process of secularization in uncovering the factors responsible for rural church decline.

At first this analysis may seem comforting to churches, since it suggests that their decline (at least in rural areas) resulted more from misplaced ideology in the context of depopulation than from some progressive loss of faith. Yet it may soon be realized that churches have not altogether lost their ideological rivalries (of which tensions between mainstream churches and the House Church Movement are a current example), and that they do still separately cover depopulated rural areas. Further, explanations which rely upon demography may eventually prove just as relativistic as those which presume an ineluctable process of secularization.

For many theologians relativism is precisely what the sociological study of earliest Christianity and the sociological study of biblical interpretation involves. In the seventh chapter I will attempt to draw out from this some of the features that present the most serious challenges to the foundations of modern theology. I will attempt to show this by tracing the path of a key New Testament text through a variety of differing social contexts. It soon becomes evident that the latter radically affect the interpretation of biblical texts and *pericope* and heighten a sense of relativism. It is not simply that meanings change somewhat over the ages and in differing social contexts. Rather it is that such mutually contradictory and opposite interpretations emerge from this form of study that the whole enterprise of building theology on biblical foundations appears to be called into question. A thoroughly sociological approach proves much more uncomfortable for biblical hermeneutics than is often imagined. Hermeneutics appears to be culture bound and socially relative.

This chapter will also refer to another area of recent theology which has been particularly open to sociological scrutiny, namely the study of ordained ministry. In part this study has come from sociologists of religion who happen to be interested in the phenomenon of ordained ministry. Those sociologists studying secularization have often shown such an interest, frequently regarding the clergy as exemplars of some process of secularization. Most recently it has been theologians who have made extensive use of sociological methods to understand the history and present patterns of ordained ministry. I will argue that it is some of this research by theologians which is the most challenging and which again heightens a sense of relativism. Indeed, relativism may actually be greater than that anticipated by critical theologians such as Schillebeeckx.

The work of all of these chapters is preparatory. Theologians have usually regarded relativism as an enemy, as a corrosive perspective which eats into the subject matter of theology and undercuts its very basis. Relativism and reductionism have frequently been confused and the social sciences, as apparent agents of both, have long been regarded with deep suspicion in some theological circles. These chapters are offered as a challenge to these theological confusions and suspicions. A heightened sense of relativism (but not necessarily reductionism) does seem to result from applying sociological methods to various aspects of theology and the churches. Whether all theologians like it or not these methods are increasingly entering the discipline of theology and especially New Testament studies. Theological protests or disdain are hardly likely to halt this trend or to stem the sense of relativism that it bears. Religious convictions do appear more relative after the introduction of sociological method than they did before.

Even those who are most disdainful of social or cultural relativism are changed by a knowledge of its possibility. Someone with strong religious or ideological convictions, who exists wholly within an enclave of others with similar convictions, differs significantly from someone with apparently similar convictions, but who is surrounded by a pluralistic environment of competing convictions. Biblical literalism provides an obvious example of this. In previous ages, when Christians generally assumed the literal truth of the apparent historical claims of the Bible, it would have been considered to be a perfectly intelligent activity to compute the age of the world from biblical genealogies. Intelligent creationist fundamentalists still make such computations today. Yet they do so in the knowledge that their activity is regarded as eccentric and deviant by many others and they are aware that their very activity constitutes a challenge to prevailing scientific orthodoxies. Their actions appear similar to those of earlier Christians, even though their attitude towards these actions is radically changed. It is changed precisely by their knowledge that such literalistic beliefs are minority beliefs in a pluralistic society. Or to express this epigrammatically, prejudices that are unchallenged are blind prejudices, whereas those which dismiss legitimate challenges are wilful prejudices.

It is possible, then, for theologians to question the propriety of applying a sociological perspective to church structures, to the New

Testament or to the history and functions of ordained ministry. It is distinctly more difficult for them to avoid the relativizing effects of these applications. Once they are aware that other theologians are using sociology in this way, the status of their own claims about churches, about the New Testament or about ordained ministry are inevitably changed. So, once Schillebeeckx's socio-historical analysis of *ordo* and *ordinatio* is known,[5] ontological claims about ordained ministry become claims against the analysis as well as claims about ministry. Or, once Shaw's socio-political analysis of Paul's claims to apostolicity are known,[6] a purely theological interpretation of these claims becomes itself an assertion of theology over-and-against this socio-political analysis.

In any case, those theologians who are most dismissive of sociology are apt to make assumptions about social determination when analysing opposing view-points. In several places in this book it will be noted how often forms of social analysis have been used by theologians past and present as means of discounting opposing views. Thus, those who ostensibly reject a positive use of sociology within theology have still tended to use forms of sociology polemically. Current polemics about ordained ministry well illustrate this point. It is not simply those challenging ontological claims about ordained ministry who adopt sociological perspectives. Those defending these claims against, for instance, the movement for the ordination of women are just as likely to use forms of social analysis, typically depicting the movement as a product of secular liberalism.

It will be argued later that these polemical uses of sociology are fundamentally flawed. A greater awareness of the genetic fallacy should persuade theologians that this is so. My point for the moment is only that these uses belie the disdain of sociology by some theologians. Perhaps what the latter really fear is that sociology tends to relativize convictions. And in this respect they are surely correct. Sociology even relativizes the convictions of those who claim certainties to counter the relativism that it fosters. The claiming of certainties does not in itself eliminate suspicions of relativism. It may even serve to reinforce these suspicions, especially when antagonistic theological factions claim differing and competing certainties. In drawing attention to this, sociology again heightens a sense of relativism.

What at first appears to be a threat to theology might eventually be recognized as a consequence of an adequate concept of theism. Far from theologians seeking to counter social and cultural relativism, they might come to see that relativism is actually required by theology if it is to be properly understood. I will argue that a mature Christianity requires us to recognize Christian pluralism as the inevitable product of a common relationship to God in Christ which is finally beyond words. An understanding of Christian faith which is relational, rather than propositional, need no longer feel intimidated by social and cultural relativism. Rather it may be seen that propositional knowledge, in the form of creeds, dogmas, or sacred scriptures, can never capture a theistic relationship which is beyond language.

On the one hand, it will be maintained that propositional knowledge does have an important function in establishing and reinforcing religious identity and differentiation. The function of the professional theologian is crucial to this. On the other hand, it will be argued that it is a theological error to confuse such propositional knowledge with the theistic relationship itself. Once this relationship assumes the central role in Christian faith, and indeed in a theology which attempts to articulate intelligently this faith, propositional knowledge will be properly viewed always as partial and relative. An expression of faith will not be confused with the theistic relationship upon which it is based. Rather it will be seen as a vital, but transient and culture bound, attempt to articulate what finally goes beyond articulation.

This relational understanding of theology will emerge only slowly. It will be offered as a theological alternative both to the forms of fundamentalism and sectarianism analysed in the next two chapters and to the competing convictions of Victorian churches analysed in the following three chapters. Then it will be set in the context of the cultural relativism within modern theology that emerges from the seventh chapter. However, it will be in the final chapter that it is explored most positively. This strategy is intentional. It is only when the full extent of relativism actually within Christianity is recognized that the point of viewing theology as a social system makes sense. By outlining a way in which theology can properly be seen as a social system, I hope to show that relative convictions are neither as absurd nor as reductionist as they might at first appear.

A full account of theology viewed as a social system must wait for a later date. For the moment it is sufficient to attempt to establish the grounds for such a system and to outline a shape that it might take. The outline presented in the final chapter is offered as a positive response to the sense of relativism so evident in the previous chapters. It seeks to show that sociological stimulus may yet help theologians to see their own task more clearly.

PART ONE

Sects and Competing Convictions

---

2 · Fundamentalist Convictions

.

The recent rise of religious fundamentalism in the West and in the Middle East provides a curious paradox. In a situation of apparent secularism, or at least of ideological pluralism, it presents a sharp reaffirmation of doctrinal certainty of conviction. In the light of resurgent and militant fundamentalism any concept of relative convictions might appear as an example of outmoded and epiphenomenal liberalism. The religious and political passion which tends to accompany recent fundamentalism all too easily overwhelms relativist/liberal religious or political positions. The latter largely failed to predict the recent success of fundamentalism. They find difficulty in understanding or even taking seriously fundamentalist convictions, and they still too readily predict the imminent eclipse of the political and social influence of fundamentalism.

Fundamentalism is problematic for both sociologists and theologians. In this chapter I intend to show how the theories of secularization which typified the 1960s seriously misled both sociologists and theologians and reduced their ability to predict or understand the rise of fundamentalism. The demise or privatization of religious thinking, practices and institutions which was thought to characterize some ineluctable process of secularization in urban industrial society now seems less obvious. A new generation of social historians, sociologists and theologians has, as a result (*inter alia*) of the resurgence of fundamentalism, become more sceptical of such models of secularization. In different ways they are beginning to challenge the premises underlying these models and to treat fundamentalism more seriously. The latter is no longer regarded simply as a temporary aberration which will soon pass. Instead, it is seen as evidence that thoroughgoing secularization models may be misleading heuristic devices.

To complete the paradox, once fundamentalism is taken seriously by critical scholarship it is also relativized, and thereby undermined, in the process. If thoroughgoing secularization models now appear misleading in the context of resurgent fundamentalism, more recent, and apparently more sympathetic, sociological and theological accounts reveal fundamentalist convictions to be themselves plural-istic and relative to specific and changing social contexts. Far from providing counter-evidence to a theory of relative convictions, they actually supply an illuminating example of the relativist challenge facing all theological convictions in a sociologically conscious world. And, precisely because modern fundamentalism is a deliberate attempt to counter this world, it is all the more vulnerable to sociological inspection. The latter's insistent probing into the social origins, maintenance, variability and social fragility of fundamental-ism, is more damaging to fundamentalist convictions than to relative convictions. Sociologists have had much success in undermining religious, ideological or political claims to certainty, even the claims to certainty periodically made by sociologists themselves. Since certainty is so crucial to fundamentalists – certainty steadfastly maintained in a manifestly uncertain world – sociological methods appear all the more damaging to their cause.

In seeking to set out the two sides of this paradox it will be necessary to agree first on a definition of fundamentalism. Unfortun-ately the term has been used so widely in the media as well as in academic circles that its meaning is far from clear. In setting out the alternative sociological and theological definitions it will soon become apparent that each tends to include some groups which are widely thought to be fundamentalist and to exclude others. Some choice is inevitable and it would be foolish to claim for any definition that it is *the* definition. Definitions are but tools for analysis. However, in the present context I will argue that it is most desirable to find a definition which both those who depict themselves as fun-damentalists and those who wish simply to study fundamentalism could adopt. Only so can the arbitrary sociological practice of im-posing labels upon others, which they personally reject, be avoided.

I

The term 'fundamentalism' first used, according to some scholars, in 1920 by an American Baptist paper to depict 'those ready to do battle royal for the Fundamentals of Protestantism',[1] finds its origins in the series of twelve booklets entitled *The Fundamentals*[2] issued between 1910 and 1915. *Ab initio*, although often adopted as a term of abuse by critics of fundamentalism, it has continuously been used as a means of self-identification by American (and less frequently British) Protestant fundamentalists themselves. Unusually the term continues to be widely used by both groups. In contrast, few religious groups identify themselves as 'sects' or 'cults'. The perjorative overtones inherent in the popular usage of these terms seems to preclude them from doing so. For example, although Mormons, Christian Scientists and Jehovah's Witnesses all might be regarded as 'sects' by society at large, members of each of these movements habitually refer to them as 'churches'. Occasionally – as with the Quakers and later the Shakers – a movement will adopt an originally somewhat derisory sobriquet as one way of referring to itself to the outside world. However, the term 'fundamentalism' is very much more than that. In origin it is a term coined in defiance of the perceived 'modernism' of the mainline denominations in the United States and is still used by American Protestant fundamentalists as a primary means of self-identification in a context of 'modernism' and 'liberalism'. If anything the secular perjorative use of the term 'fundamentalism' has strengthened its use as a primary means of self-identification amongst fundamentalists. It is thus at once a cultural and a counter-cultural term in its use in the West.

'Fundamentalism' is also used as a cultural and a counter-cultural term within present-day Islam. In an important study, originally made for the United States government in its attempt to understand resurgent Islamic fundamentalism, R. Hrair Dekmejian contrasts the various terms used outside and within Islam to depict this phenomenon:

> The heightening of Islamic consciousness has been variously characterized as revivalism, rebirth, puritanism, fundamentalism, reassertion, awakening, reformism, resurgence, renewal, renaissance, revitalization, militancy, activism, millenarianism, messianism, return to Islam, and the march of Islam. Collectively, these terms are useful in describing the complexity of the Islamic phenomenon; yet they impute a certain dormancy to Islam, which does not conform to reality. In point of fact, Islam has successfully resisted the encapsulation imposed upon Christianity in the West – a resistance that is at the core of the ongoing conflict between state and religion in the Islamic world. Thus, it is

instructive to review terms and constructs in the original Arabic usage regarding the Islamic revolution. Proponents and sympathizers frequently use the following expressions: *bath al Islami* (Islamic renaissance), *sahwah al-Islamiyyah* (Islamic awakening), *ihya al-Din* (Religious revival) *al-usuliyyah al-Islamiyyah* (Islamic fundamentalism). The most appropriate term is *al-usuliyyah al Islamiyyah* since it connotes a search for the fundamentals of the faith, the foundations of the Islamic polity (*ummah*), and the bases of legitimate authority (*al-shariyyah al-hukm*).[3]

Dekmejian is at pains to stress the continuity of the present-day resurgence of Islamic fundamentalism with periodic Islamic revivals since the Prophet died. Similarly James Barr in his studies of Christian fundamentalism[4] has traced its roots to the eighteenth rather than to the twentieth century. Nonetheless most sociological accounts of present-day fundamentalism also wish to stress its specifically modern features. Both Dekmejian and Barr are aware that it is a counter-cultural phenomenon at odds with modernity. If the latter is emphasized, fundamentalism, however rooted in past revivalism, is identified as a specifically twentieth-century phenomenon. It is seen as a form, or varying forms, of religious response to the 'relativism' and 'liberalism' of modernity. Both Shi'ite fundamentalists in present-day Iran (identifying 'modernity' as 'Westernization') and Southern Baptist fundamentalists in the United States might be happy to see themselves in these counter-cultural terms. They would not of course agree on the substantive contents of their respective religious responses to modernity. Yet their understandings of modernity and their determinations to oppose its perceived effects through religious means have many points in common.

The concept of 'modernity' is itself elusive and there is considerable debate amongst sociologists about both its meaning and its relationship to urbanization, industrialization and especially to secularization.[5] Without being side-tracked into this debate, it is still possible to see that the 'modern world' (for convenience 'modernity'), or at least the effects of modernity, are frequently the object of attack from self-styled fundamentalists, even when they are expert exponents of modern technology. The irony, for example, of critics of the media using the media to disseminate their criticisms, is certainly not limited to religious fundamentalists. Yet the latter, especially in the United States, have been amongst the most successful in exploiting de-regulated commercial television. In Iran, too, public television has been extensively used as a medium of fundamentalist control. And, the Iran–Iraq war saw the first protracted confrontation to use the most recent war technology. It even supplied an 'invaluable' source of field information about the strategic capabilities of this technology for those industrialized nations manufacturing it. Despite the rhetoric of many fundamentalists against modernity, their actual opposition to it is selective. Similarly, although anti-evolutionary creationism has typified many American Southern Baptist fundamentalists, they have frequently sought to justify this through scientific means.

In his introduction to a recent collection of studies on Islamic resurgence, Ernest Gellner seeks to depict the relationship between this resurgence and modernity. He argues that 'the introduction of the new and very powerful productive, military and administrative technology has a number of consequences, amongst which the one most relevant for our purposes is the erosion of the small subcommunities which were *the* essential cells of social life in the traditional situation'.[6] An immediate consequence of the new technology has been a considerable increase in the complexity of the division of labour and a greatly enhanced power of the central state. A tribal society allowing for private vengeance and communal military self-help has given way to a modern, technologically based state. Durkheimian religious communities have lost their central role. Old forms of the sacred 'had once ratified and sustained and oiled social forms which have disappeared or are disappearing. So their function vanishes, only their personnel, and their doctrinal rationale, remains'.[7] Present-day Islamic fundamentalism fills this vacuum and is better adapted to the new urban order (whilst still being deeply rooted in the historic past of the Muslim community):

> The new style enables the recently urbanised rustics simultaneously to disavow their rural past, of which they are openly ashamed, and to express their resentment of their opulent and questionably orthodox rulers, whom they secretly envy. Thus, one and the same style, serves simultaneously to define a new emergent Muslim nationality against the foreigner, to provide a charter for self-disciplining and a disavowal of past weakness, for the elevation of rustics into townsmen, and for a critical stance towards the rulers, one which the latter cannot easily disregard . . . So is there a mystery about the social bases of the puritanical, scripturalist Reformism which has swept Islam?[8]

Gellner clearly believes that there is not. Other Middle East specialists interpret the situation slightly differently. Dekmejian

ignores rural/urban transitions in the Islamic world and sees the rise
of fundamentalism as the result of a combination of a charismatic
leadership and political crisis (notably the 1967 Arab defeat). For
him military and economic modernization has rather caused a clash
of values: 'whilst the modernists are inclined toward the wholesale
emulation of Western social theory and practice, most traditional-
ists advocate the selective borrowing of aspects of Western experience thought to be compatible with Islam, i.e., science and
technology'.[9] And Sami Zubaida's analysis of the social composi-
tion of fundamentalists also seems to differ from that of Gellner:

> The main activists in the Islamic movements in both Egypt and
> Iran are the young intelligentsia, which may be termed the
> intellectual proletariat of students, teachers and minor functio-
> naries, together with some elements drawn from the urban
> working class and 'petty bourgeois' shopkeepers and artisans
> (these latter elements constituting a numerical minority). These
> are the same social groups from whom support is drawn for all
> oppositional politics, left and right, religious and secular. As for
> the urban poor, the indications are that their participation is
> sporadic, little organized and probably dependent on bandwagon
> effect.[10]

These varying analyses are not necessarily mutually exclusive and
it may be too early to expect clear lines to emerge in the scholarly
study of recent Islamic fundamentalism. Most see it as a response in
some form to modernism and yet as combining an ambivalent
attitude to modern technology and the Western values associated
with it. In this respect it has much in common with American
Protestant fundamentalism. This in turn may or may not be causally
related in both manifestations of fundamentalism to the urbanization of a rural community. In the context of Sunni fundamentalism,
Emmanuel Sivan argues that, especially in poorer Arab countries
where it is strong, 'the very failure of modernity to deliver upon its
promises explains the radical message'.[11] The latter may also be
peculiarly related to the Arab–Israeli political crisis of 1967
(sometimes used within the apocalyptic visions of American
fundamentalists, but certainly not a causal agency of them).[12] For
Ian Lustick it is this crisis which is central to the emergence of
Jewish fundamentalism.

Lustick relates the founding of the most militant fundamentalist
movement in Israel today Gush Emunim (literally 'the Bloc of the
Faithful') in 1974, firstly to the territorial aspirations that followed

the Six Day War in 1967 and then to the political crisis following the Yom Kippur War in 1973. He argues:

The Yom Kippur War was the first major conflict in which substantial numbers of Orthodox Jews participated within regular combat units. Famous for their knitted skullcaps, these soldiers came mainly from the recently created Yeshivot Hesder in which young religious Jews were permitted to integrate half-time study of sacred texts with regular service in the army. This participation gave religious Israeli Jews self-confidence and legitimacy within the wider secular society. Amid the psychological confusion of the period following the Yom Kippur War, a generation of young religious idealists, whose pride had always suffered by the honour granted to kibbutzniks and other secular Jews for serving in the army, felt empowered to offer their own analysis of Israel's predicament, and their own solution. But their analysis was not technocratic, it was theological. Their solution was a spiritual rejuvenation of society whose most important expression and source of strength would be settlement on and communion with the greater, liberated Land of Israel.[13]

Lustick maintains that Gush Emunim consists primarily of well-educated, middle-class Ashkenazic Israelis and has 10,000–20,000 activists. With the slogan 'The Land of Israel, for the People of Israel, According to the Torah of Israel', they have been most visible in their settlements (supported financially by Likud) in the West Bank and Gaza Strip. Indeed, 'the men and women of Gush Emunim have made it their life's work to ensure that the occupied West Bank and Gaza Strip are permanently incorporated into the State of Israel. The level and intensity of their commitment, flowing from the fundamental, even cosmic, issues they perceive to be directly at stake, had largely disappeared from Israeli politics. Their operational objective is to accelerate the pace at which the Jewish people fulfils its destiny.'[14] Religious aspirations are predominant with Gush Emunim, although Lustick points out that an important non-religious minority has also formed settlements and belongs to the movement.

The combination of fundamentalism and territorial claims and actions make Gush Emunim particularly potent in the Middle East today. Indeed, the juxtaposition of Islamic and Jewish fundamentalism has obvious implications for the peace of the world. Lustick's aims in studying Jewish fundamentalism are overtly political. He maintains that 'virtually no serious observers believe a negotiated

solution to the Arab-Israeli conflict is possible unless Jewish
fundamentalism's key goal – establishment of permanent Jewish
rule of the whole Land of Israel – is thwarted. Yet, for the
foreseeable future, the political leverage this movement and its
allies can exert will prevent the Israeli political system from
responding positively, by normal, peaceful parliamentary means, to
opportunities to achieve such an agreement, no matter how
attractive its terms.'[15] Most terrifying of all, Lustick outlines the
way some within Gush Emunim since 1983 have sought to remove
Muslim shrines from the Dome of the Rock and to re-establish the
Jewish Temple. He even quotes military sources speculating on the
possibility of fundamentalists planting explosives within the Dome
of the Rock. In the context of competing fundamentalisms such an
action might prove quite literally disastrous.

Gush Emunim is clearly still a highly fluid movement and Lustick
has some difficulty in reaching a definition of fundamentalism which
will cover it adequately. Because its members are not wholly
religious and also because his own interests are predominantly
political, he rejects specifically religious definitions of the term. He
is fully aware of the American Protestant origins of the term, but
regards etymology as finally unsatisfactory, since 'it would apply as
well to monastic sects and traditionalist religions whose rigid
enforcement of elaborate rules entails complete withdrawal from
society as to crusades designed to reorder the world according to the
dictates of the Holy Writ'.[16] Instead, he believes that what
characterizes fundamentalists is their unwillingness to engage in any
form of political pragmatism whilst seeking to implement radical
changes in society. Their political aspirations are uncompromising,
dogmatically based and comprehensive. In short, 'a belief system is
defined as fundamentalist in so far as its adherents regard its tenets
as uncompromizable and direct transcendental imperatives to
political action oriented toward the rapid and comprehensive
reconstruction of society'.[17]

Lustick is unusual, and unusually helpful, in offering a formal
definition of fundamentalism. Others characteristically group
together features which they regard as fundamentalist. Frequently
this is done by referring to the supposedly five features commended
in *The Fundamentals*: namely, biblical inerrancy, the virgin birth,
substitutionary atonement, the bodily resurrection, and the histori-
city of miracles.[18] The difficulty involved in this is that it limits
fundamentalism to Christianity and that, even within Christian
fundamentalism, it ignores the debate about whether or not other

elements (notably apocalypticism) are to be included. Christian fundamentalism *ab initio* has been internally divided on this second point. Alternatively, following Barr,[19] more analytic features are sometimes grouped together to depict fundamentalism – namely its exclusivity, oppositional character, its prominent soteriological and eschatological beliefs, its compartmentalization of religion, its ahistoricity, and its rationalistic character (this last is for Barr an important feature distinguishing present-day from earlier exclusive systems of Christian belief). Lustick goes beyond this by offering a formal definition rather an analytic description.

However his definition has obvious limitations. It takes a term developed in a religious context and removes all religious reference from it. Sometimes this is done in church-sect typology when political parties are analysed as 'church-like' or 'sect-like'. Although this can be useful, it might more properly be regarded as an analogical use of typology. It alters such typology very considerably if instead politics becomes its primary reference. Perhaps Lustick dismisses etymology too easily. Again, his definition would seem to cover such movements as economic monetarism (if strongly and radically held) and exclude rigid religious groups which withdraw from society. Indeed, Lustick regards it as a virtue of his definition that it is able to include secular members of Gush Emunim and exclude ultra-orthodox Jewish groups in Israel, the Haredim. Yet, on this understanding, self-styled American Protestant fundamentalists can be regarded as 'fundamentalist' only if they are also politically active – which, until very recently, they have seldom been. Those who claim to be fundamentalist, but do not participate in political movements such as Moral Majority, are to be excluded by definition, whereas non-religious but bigoted political activists who make no claim to fundamentalism are to be included. Of course definitions are but tools for analysis, but it is possible that Lustick's is too specifically related to a particular context for wider application.

Before suggesting an alternative definition, it is necessary first to isolate those features which the various groups who refer to themselves as fundamentalists (across religious traditions) seem to have in common. If this is to be achieved these features clearly cannot be specifically related to Christian doctrines. For this reason more general analytic features are to be preferred. Yet they must be sufficiently religious and sufficiently distinct within religious systems if they are meaningfully to depict present-day fundamentalism. Ideally they should also have some relationship to the original use of the term: etymology should at least be taken seriously.

Two general features of fundamentalism might be isolated – the first cognitive and the second sociological. At a cognitive level, fundamentalism can be seen as a series of movements committed to scriptural absolutism. And, at a sociological level, it can be seen as a series of counter-cultures, that is, as movements consciously opposed to the pluralism and relativism that appear to accompany modernity. In fundamentalism these two features are intimately related: scriptural absolutism is upheld as a counter to modernity and defines the varying counter-cultural forms that fundamentalism assumes.

The notion of scriptural absolutism does not simply involve a high view of scripture which characterizes many evangelical forms of Christianity and most of Islam and orthodox Judaism. Even the notion of scriptural inerrancy is too wide, since it is possible to believe that scripture is inerrant but in need of supplementation and further, but optional, interpretation. Rather scripture (and additional, but non-optional, interpretations of scripture) is regarded as *the* resource to guide the modern world and as *the* source for imperatives about how the modern world is to be changed. Scriptural absolutism regards with disdain historical/critical scriptural scholarship and anathematizes any approaches to scripture which are anything less than absolute.

Counter-culture is clearly present in this understanding of scriptural absolutism. Without serious competitors various forms of Christianity, Islam and Judaism have of course been literalistic at times in their understanding of scripture. Yet it would be an anachronism to call this fundamentalism. Self-styled fundamentalism has in addition been characterized by a systematic attempt to counter scriptural relativism. Within American fundamentalism this takes the form of frequent attacks upon liberal Protestantism and biblical criticism. The latter are viewed as the typical products of a relativist, liberal and permissive society. And it is just such a society, they would argue, which allows the film *The Last Temptation of Christ* to be shown to the public. With some sociological justice a link is presumed between modernity and pluralism: modern technology and systems of communication inevitably create a level of cultural pluralism and consequent relativism hitherto unknown.[20] Within Islamic fundamentalism an attack upon scriptural relativism and upon pluralistic modernity is just as apparent. In this respect the attack upon Salman Rushdie's *The Satanic Verses* was not an aberration. Shi'ite fundamentalism in Iran in 1979 was very consciously an attempt to reverse the evil cultural effects of modernity and to place in its stead a society founded upon Islamic scripture. Sunni fundamentalism in Egypt has been characterized by a sustained attack on 'permissive' modernity and an attempt to replace it with a greater adherence to scripture. And within Judaism, even the ostensibly non-religious minority of Gush Emunim are party to territorial demands based upon scriptural absolutism. Some analysts would also include as fundamentalists militant Sikhs' use of Guru Granth Sahib and Sri Lankan Tamil worshippers of Siva's use of Agamic canons.[21]

Counter-culture based upon scriptural absolutism is also a feature of some religious groups – within Christianity, Islam and Judaism – that withdraw from the world. Some of these seek to build the purest form of counter-culture which avoids unnecessary contact with the contaminating world. There is no reason why their political quietism should exclude them from being regarded as fundamentalist. On the other hand, purely political groups or even counter-cultural religious groups which are not characterized by scriptural absolutism (e.g. the followers of Archbishop LeFebre) can, on this understanding, only be termed 'fundamentalist' by analogy. This may not be a disadvantage since they would not usually use the term to depict themselves. It may not be possible finally to find an exact match between groups that can be analytic-ally identified as fundamentalist and groups that regard themselves as fundamentalist,[22] but the closer the match the better.

With all of these points in mind, fundamentalism may be tentatively defined as a system of beliefs and practices which treat scriptural absolutism as *the* way to counter the pluralism and relativism engendered by modernity. And the term militant fun-damentalism might be used further to distinguish those recent forms of fundamentalism which have sought actively to counter modernity through political means.

II

So defined it is hardly surprising that Western social scientists, religionists and theologians largely failed to predict the recent resurgences of fundamentalism and have been slow to take them seriously. Counter-cultural scriptural absolutism is so antithetical to the presumptions that predominate in Western scholarship, that the Shi'ite revolution in Iran in 1979 and the political role of the Moral Majority in the American elections in the 1980s are only slowly being adequately assessed. Gradually it is being realized in several parts of the scholarly world that they represent a challenge to the consensus about secularization that dominated the 1960s. It was a consensus that predominated amongst historians, sociologists, political theorists, religionists and also theologians. Even those few critics of secularization models in the 1960s largely failed to foresee a resurgence of counter-cultural scriptural absolutism.

Dekmejian (writing in 1985) well expresses the situation in the scholarly West:

> The Western practice of placing Islamic fundamentalism under the rubric of 'fanaticism' is singularly dysfunctional to a balanced and dispassionate analysis of the subject. Indeed, to a Western world preoccupied with growing economic problems and security concerns, the Islamic challenge was unexpected and ominous. Few in the non-Islamic sphere were able to anticipate an Islamic resurgence in the modern context. The conceptual myopia induced by Western and Marxist materialism had effectively blindfolded both scholars and statesmen, who tended to dismiss or underestimate the regenerative capacity of Islam.[23]

Of course there is still considerable debate amongst scholars about the durability of this resurgence and about the extent and political importance of militant Protestant fundamentalism within the United States. However this debate does not detract from Dekmejian's argument. The present resurgence of militant fundamentalism (however long it lasts) was largely unforeseen[24] and is only now being taken seriously within the scholarly world.

To understand why this has been so, it is instructive to compare the secularization models that predominated in the 1960s with those that are emerging in various scholarly fields today. Elsewhere[25] I have analysed at length the influential writings of Bryan Wilson[26] in Britain and Peter Berger[27] in the United States on secularization. It is unnecessary to rehearse this analysis in full here and, in any case, I will return to part of Wilson's theory in chapter 4. Rather the equally influential *The Decline of the Sacred in Industrial Society*[28] by the Italian S. S. Acquaviva (published originally in Milan in 1966) can serve to represent this genre within the sociology of religion.

Acquaviva's intention was to examine the religious crisis that he believed accompanies industrialization. To do this he first examined available statistical data from Europe, Britain and the United States and then turned to more cultural considerations. For him the statistical/structural decline of the churches that his data suggested was related, but at a slight distance, to the demise of cognitive forms of religiosity in society. Thus, 'as secularization advances in industrial and post-industrial society, the traditional "sacred cosmos" loses its significance as the index of a religiosity bound up with the experience of the sacred. This is because of the high degree of subjectivization of models of belief'.[29] In other words, as the ecclesial basis of religiosity diminishes as an accompaniment of industrialization, religious belief, if it survives at all, becomes more private and idiosyncratic. Further, irreligiosity grows in such a society, especially amongst those who are best educated. This represents a radical departure from previous ages:

> In the centuries prior to our own, religiosity – at least externally, and with only marginal exceptions – was universal. The abandonment of religion was then no more than the passage from one religion to another, and not a shift from religion to atheism. Those who never engaged in any sort of religious practice were very few indeed, and locally could usually be picked out by name . . . To this near unanimity of practice there corresponded a fairly unanimous religiosity on the past of the individual: social life was shot through with religious significance. It is widely accepted that in the early stages of human history the structure of society was thoroughly pervaded by religious conceptions.[30]

It is clear that twentieth-century industrialized society is quite different and that religion seems to have lost much of this unanimity and socio-structural role. Secularization, in Acquaviva's analysis, affects church structures, it affects 'the attribution of sacred significance . . . to things, persons, spaces, etc.', and it affects 'the attribution of sacred significance to behaviour (moral, etc.)'.[31] It does not necessarily entail the total disappearance of religion, but it has changed religious conviction within society:

> One might maintain the thesis that in industrial society, the sacred and the religious tend more and more to become a sort of unexpressed potentiality instead of the active, manifest elements that they were until relatively recently . . . Our review of the various levels of inquiry relevant to the problem of religion in contemporary society, do not allow us to say where the process of secularization will terminate, or whether there will be any substantial reversal of the current tendency. All that can be said with certainty is that the decline of the sacred is intimately connected with the changes in society and human psychology. It cannot be considered as merely a contingent fact: it is associated

with the collapse, whether temporarily or finally, of traditions, cultures, and values. From the religious point of view, humanity has entered a long night that will become darker and darker with the passing of the generations, and of which no end can yet be seen. It is a night in which there seems to be no place for a conception of God, or for a sense of the sacred, and ancient ways of giving significance to our own existence, of confronting life and death, are becoming increasingly untenable. At bottom, the motivation for religious behaviour and for faith persists – the need to explain ourselves and what surrounds us, the anguish, and the sense of precariousness. But man remains uncertain whether somewhere there exists, or ever existed, something different from uncertainty, doubt, and existential insecurity.[32]

Acquaviva's analysis is far from crude. This passage alone shows theological as well as sociological sensitivity. The church statistics that he used are indeed crude by more recent standards (for instance, he frequently drew conclusions about church decline from single decade statistics). Further his, and others', sweeping contrast between the twentieth century and the 'golden age' of religion in the past has been subjected to considerable criticism.[33] Nevertheless, he did not claim that secularization is some ineluctable process: this is not social determinism. Nor did he ignore more privatized forms of religiosity. Yet having conceded that, there is nothing in his analysis which would make imminent resurgences of militant fundamentalism in heavily industrialized societies even remotely feasible. Counter-cultural scriptural absolutism should not have been a viable option for people within burgeoning industrial societies if his analysis was correct. And it certainly should not have been a viable option for an educated urban élite in the 1980s within the Arab world.[34]

The extent to which scholars have changed, as the result of such disconfirmatory evidence, can be gauged by examining recent collections of essays on religion and society from social historians, political scientists, and sociologists. And within theology, the recent writings of Harvey Cox, such a pivotal figure in the secularization debate in the 1960s, represent a very remarkable shift of position.

Disciplines of Faith: Studies in Religion, Politics and Patriarchy[35] found its origins in the Religion and Society History Workshop meeting of 1983 in London. The editors are aware that their 'recognition of the power of religion as a shaping force of politics in the contemporary world . . . is uncomfortable for socialists who have traditionally anticipated the eventual triumph of reason over superstition, as it is for sociologists with their paradigms of secularization and rationalization, allegedly characteristic of the modern world'.[36] Yet they argue that in a wide variety of situations in the modern world – Iran, Northern Ireland, Israel, Poland and the United States – this power is evident.

The editors of this large collection, to which I shall return later,[37] then point to the remarkable political changes that have taken place recently within the Roman Catholic world. In particular, they highlight the rise of liberation theology in South America, Christian–Marxist dialogue, and the shift to the left of much Western Catholicism. All of this, they argue, fits uncomfortably with traditional socialist and sociological interpretations of the demise of religion in modern society.

In another recent collection, *The Political Role of Religion in the United States*,[38] a mixture of sociologists and political scientists are similarly convinced that resurgences of religiosity in the modern world require greater attention from specialists. In similar tones to the first collection, the editors of the second begin their introduction as follows:

> To many social scientists the current burst of political activity by religious leaders that we have witnessed in the later 1970s and early 1980s has come as a surprise. A dominant scholarly thesis had been that modern-day society trends, such as the cultural diversity of the American people and the increased use of science to solve today's problems, had brought greater secularization in all of our lives. Secularization is a system of ideas and practices that disregards or rejects any form of religious faith or worship. But despite these long-term secular trends, we have recently seen in the United States, and indeed around the world, the resurgence of religion into the secular sphere of the political arena.[39]

They then proceed to point to all the same instances of resurgence cited by the editors of *Disciplines of Faith*. The two collections, it should be noted, were written quite independently, the first from Britain and the second from the United States. The editors of the second collection, however, are still convinced that there is apparent a process of secularization. This process is evident for them in the cultural effects of technology and science, in the rise of humanism, in the dominance of economic systems and in the increasing privatization of religion. Without detracting from this they conclude:

> This analysis of secular trends would seem to justify the conclusions that religious influence in modern life is weak and that those who attempt to change this condition will find it to be no easy task. The remarkable feature of the eighties, however, is that churches have increasingly taken up the challenge presented by secularization. The response of the religious institution is twofold. On the one hand, there are those leaders who resist the changes associated with modernity or modern secular trends. These are mainly the Christian Rightists. On the other hand, there are those leaders and institutions that more or less accept modernity and try to adjust, not necessarily accommodate, to the new situation. These are the liberal Catholics, Protestants, and Jews.[40]

A third recent collection, this time specifically sociological in orientation, *The Sacred in a Secular Age*,[41] ought also to be mentioned. In the light of the dominance of thoroughgoing secularization models in the 1960s, the most remarkable feature of this collection is that only one of its contributors, Bryan Wilson, appears to hold an unmodified position on secularization. The editor, Phillip Hammond, cites three sets of data which have been responsible for this modification: the resurgences of fundamentalism; the persistence of 'popular', 'folk' or 'unofficial' religion in the modern world (there is still much dispute about how to label this phenomenon, characterized as it is by only very loose connections with institutional forms of religions);[42] and the continuing role of religion within political/military conflicts in Northern Ireland and the Middle East.

Perhaps the most surprising group of social scientists to note a resurgence of religiosity in the modern world is geographers. Amongst them the phenomenon of pilgrimage is attracting increasing attention. A session of the 83rd Annual Meeting of the Association of American Geographers concentrated upon this subject with scholars contributing from both North America and West Germany. In the collection that resulted the editors noted in their introduction:

> Pilgrimages to holy places have taken place since early days in the history of mankind. They, however, attained great significance with the emergence and development of the great world religions

(Hinduism, Buddhism, Judaism, Christianity and Islam). They may be considered among the oldest forms of circulation based upon non-economic factors, although they were greatly facilitated by the contemporary trade routes . . . Despite a general tendency toward secularization in the modern world and other religious changes, pilgrimages have been experiencing a world-wide boom during the last few decades, thanks to the modern means of mass transportation and the increasing use of the automobile. The World Christian Encyclopaedia (1982) estimates that altogether about 130 million people take part in pilgrimages every year.[43]

There are problems in treating all pilgrimages uncritically as manifestations of religious resurgence. For instance it has proved extremely difficult to distinguish adequately between pilgrimages and tourism and to be clear about the motivation of all those visiting pilgrim shrines in the modern world (and perhaps the mediaeval world too). Nevertheless, within Europe especially, the very considerable interest in pilgrim shrines today seems to these geographers to point to a resurgence of popular Catholicism. And the latter seems to run counter to 'a general tendency toward secularization in the modern world'.

Critical theologians have in general been only selectively interested in these apparent manifestations of religious resurgence. Liberation theology and the political shifts within Western Catholicism have received very considerable attention. The resurgence of fundamentalism and the persistence (and perhaps even growth, as apparent in the popularity of New Age literature) of 'unofficial' religion have received scant theological attention. If fundamentalism is identified as counter-cultural scriptural absolutism it is not difficult to see why this is so. It is as antithetical to the ethos of critical theology as the idiosyncrasies of New Age religiosity. The theoretical, critical and political orientation of liberation theology has interested and challenged theologians throughout the Western world. The lack of theoretical sophistication or critical self-inspection, combined in many instances (but not of course in Islamic fundamentalism) with right-wing political orientations, seems to have repelled most theologians from taking fundamentalism or 'unofficial' religion seriously.[44] In this respect Harvey Cox's recent *Religion in the Secular City*[45] is an important exception.

Cox's original contribution to the secularization debate in the 1960s, *The Secular City*,[46] was extremely influential at the time. It was one of the most forthright defences of the theological opportunities offered by secularization. Ten years after it was written, I argued[47] that its sociological understanding of secularization was considerably deficient. I maintained that secularization was a far more ambiguous process, or set of processes, than had often been construed by sociologists and theologians in the 1960s. In *Religion in the Secular City* Cox reverses many of his previous arguments about secularization and maintains instead that 'postmodern' theology must come to terms with the resurgences of religion in the modern world apparent in both liberation theology and fundamentalism. Undoubtedly his sympathies and interests lie more with liberation theology,[48] but, unusually amongst theologians, he does give considerable attention to American Protestant fundamentalism (although very little to Islamic or Jewish fundamentalism).

It is not simply the large popular support that American Protestant fundamentalism apparently receives today that attracts Cox's attention. He argues that there are deeper theological reasons for taking fundamentalism seriously:

> When theologians do pay attention to fundamentalism, they often misunderstand it. They tend to examine it as a somewhat bizarre variant of Protestantism. Most fail to recognize it not only as a theology, but also as the faith of an identifiable subculture and as an ideology. The rudiments of a postmodern theology will emerge from Christian subcultures that have been in touch with the dominant liberal theological consensus of the modern world but have not been absorbed by it. The American fundamentalist movement qualifies as such a subculture.[49]

The theological challenge of fundamentalism for Cox resides in its location as a subculture (I believe that the term 'counter-culture' is actually more accurate) and as an ideology. It is a religious challenge to modernity. Finally Cox concludes that it is also a flawed challenge to modernity: 'beginning as an intellectual movement that quickly developed a grass-roots following but had articulate scholarly defenders, it has become an élite-led phenomenon which – with some important exceptions – displays relatively little interest in intellectual questions. Starting as a ferociously antimodernist movement, it has recently embraced some of the most questionable features of the modern world its founders despised'.[50] It is for these reasons that Cox prefers the subcultural 'base communities' which have received their focus in South American liberation theology.

Not all of this theological critique fits Islamic and Jewish forms of fundamentalism. Indeed, in so far as various forms of Shi'ite and Sunni fundamentalism have grass-roots, radical, and subcultural support in parts of the Muslim world, it is difficult to see why they should not qualify for Cox's approval. They even successfully combine a radical rejection of Western materialism (if not armaments) with strong religious commitment. And the rejection of élitism amongst the Sunni also seems to meet his critique. It is possible that Cox's own critique of modernity and modern theology in *Religion in the Secular City* is more vulnerable to the Islamic fundamentalist example than he realizes.

This issue apart, Cox's dramatic shift from *The Secular City* to *Religion in the Secular City* over the last two decades is an important indicator of changed attitudes to secularization. If the first book largely applauds modernity and welcomes the opportunities provided by thoroughgoing secularization, the second is deeply critical of modernity and sceptical about the pervasiveness of secularization. In both instances Cox accurately reflects the predominant (but of course mutually contradictory) assumptions amongst social scientists and historians within these separate decades. Militant fundamentalism (amongst other signs of religious resurgence) is now being taken seriously by scholars who must largely find its tenets distasteful. Even theologians who have been nurtured on scriptural criticism are slowly being forced to pay attention to fundamentalist claims and convictions.

III

Herein lies the challenge to a theological concept of relative convictions. Resurgent fundamentalism seems to provide a startling counter-demonstration, even within heavily industrialized, urban society, of absolutist convictions. The scriptural absolutism that is essential to it appears untempered by the relativism of a pluralist society. Indeed, this scriptural absolutism is used as *the* means to challenge, judge and change modernity and its accompanying relativism and pluralism. For the millions of fundamentalists world-wide any concept of relative convictions must appear as anathema and as a part of the modernity that is to be countered through absolutist appeals to scripture.

Yet, even within this expression of the fundamentalist challenge lie the seeds of its scholarly undermining. Because fundamentalism is widely seen to be a feature not just of parts of Christianity but also of Islam and Judaism (and possibly of other traditions too) in the

1980s, it has proved necessary to define it in terms that are not solely Christian. The term 'scriptural' absolutism has been adopted precisely for this reason. It is not simply the Bible (itself, of course, a contentious term for Christians and Jews) which is the object of this absolutism, it is a number of distinct and mutually-exclusive scriptures. By observing this the sociologist will inevitably conclude that the resultant absolutist convictions seem to be similar only in form not in content. Further by subjecting their differing contents to comparative analysis the sociologist appears thereby to relativize them.

This process of sociological relativization is applicable even to the fundamentalism of a single religious tradition. It has already been pointed out that one of the limitations of defining Christian fundamentalism in terms of the supposedly five doctrinal claims of *The Fundamentals* of 1910–15, is that fundamentalists themselves cannot agree on the five. In other words, *ab initio* pluralism was apparent within Christian fundamentalism. It is even more apparent when Christian fundamentalism is also studied in its modern extensions into the non-Western world. This becomes abundantly clear in the social anthropologist Lionel Caplan's recent study of Christian fundamentalism in Madras. In this context, Christian fundamentalism has distinct similarities to Hinduism. Caplan argues:

> Despite what some scholars might regard as a wide ontological chasm between them, and the extremely harsh judgments of Hinduism by Protestant pietists and fundamentalists alike, at the phenomenological level, at least, there would appear to be a wide measure of overlap. For people of both 'faiths' the world is populated by a host of malificent forces – human or superhuman – which must either be avoided, or against which the protection of more powerful, benign beings must be sought. In accord with this conception, both traditions have recourse to a divine hierarchy, though one (the Hindu) consists of a number of subtle gradations, while that of Protestantism is starkly dualistic, with Jesus opposed to all the forces of malignancy. There is, thus, also a place in both for the prophet, the divinely inspired worker of miracles who is set apart from and may be seen to undermine the authority of the priestly specialist operating within prescribed textual or traditional systems of knowledge.[51]

It will come as no surprise to the critical theologian to discover that Christian scriptural absolutisms result in differing visions of

Christianity. Only a unitary understanding of the New Testament would suggest otherwise. Once the New Testament is regarded as itself pluralistic, it becomes evident that Christian fundamentalists must make choices (which they could have made differently) in their particular version of scriptural absolutism. By observing this process the sociologist tends to relativize the particular scriptural absolutism that is being observed (I will pursue this further in chapter 7). And this in itself, once adopted as a proper procedure, undermines the very absolutist convictions of fundamentalists themselves. Dispassionate comparative analysis becomes the arch-enemy of fundamentalism.

Again, as soon as differing versions of fundamentalism are compared, it becomes evident that their counter-cultural oppositions to modernity differ. In part this doubtless results from their settings in different cultures. By definition country-cultures will be affected by cultural change. So, whereas American Protestant fundamentalists have made considerable use of privatized media technology, Shi'ite fundamentalists in Iran have been more attracted to military technology. In themselves these compromises with modernity may affect them quite differently. To use commercial television effectively tele-evangelists must be careful not to alienate their major source of revenue (the television audience itself) which is essential to their continuing use of this expensive medium (Shi'ites in Iran are less susceptible since they use publicly-funded television). Sociological analysis of the practical implications of this[52] again tends to foster relativization. And sociological analysis of the counter-cultural variations within Islamic fundamentalism has a similar effect.[53] There is no single counter-cultural opposition to modernity apparent within fundamentalism. There are wide variations in political orientation (from the far right to the far left), in the acceptance or non-acceptance of technology, and in the tolerance or intolerance shown to secular art, music or literature.

The sociological observation of these variations within fundamentalism does much to undermine their absolutist claims. Of course it is still possible for individual fundamentalists to be aware of these variations, yet to continue with the belief that their convictions alone are correct. All others, even those claiming uniquely to possess the truth, are quite simply mistaken. However to maintain this belief, whilst knowing about fundamentalist variations, is already to change the belief itself. Absolutist conviction, in this instance, becomes not just a counter-cultural opposition to modernity but also an opposition to competing forms of fundamentalism. In other words, it is a claim to certainty in the context of a knowledge of competing certainties and wider scepticism. Of course fundamentalism has always reacted against the scepticism of the world at large, but now it must also react against an awareness of competing fundamentalist convictions. Steve Bruce expresses the dilemma of the modern fundamentalist epigrammatically: 'in order to resist the incursions of the modern rational world, fundamentalists must act and think like members of that world'.[54]

Sociological method produces 'knowledge' for those who adopt its procedures which is particularly damaging to the absolutist claims of fundamentalists. In the light of this method the dramatic example of resurgent fundamentalism no longer appears as counter-evidence to a theory of relative convictions. Rather it becomes an example (paradoxically) of relative convictions.

3 · Impending Convictions

The previous chapter sought to understand fundamentalism as a response to modernity and specifically to the religious and cultural pluralism that modernity tends to engender. Confronted with a social context that seems to relativize all religious and ideological convictions, fundamentalists respond with an attempt to enforce cognitive uniformity. From a theological perspective, they achieve this uniformity in Christianity only by ignoring the pluralism of the New Testament and by constructing a 'harmony' of biblical and doctrinal resources. From a sociological perspective, they do so by overcoming key moments of dissonance when their cognitive world conflicts with their social context. If fundamentalists are tempted at times to make specific and refutable predictions about the world, they are particularly vulnerable to dissonance.

Perhaps their most obvious temptation today is to make specific predictions about an impending catastrophe linked to nuclear destruction. Doubtless as the Third Millennium draws near all kinds of marginal sects – including parts of the New Age subculture – will make such predictions with an increasing use of the eschatological imagery of apocalyptic literature. Parts of the fundamentalist religious right are already linking nuclear destruction with Armageddon and the dawning of the New Heaven here on earth. Paradoxically their connections may even be prophetic. Tragically it might be religious fundamentalists – Shi'ite or Christian – who finally unleash nuclear weapons upon the world. After all, from their perspective, they have the least reasons for fearing the consequences of nuclear war. God is good and will protect or reward them for their courage. They, unlike the pragmatic bureaucracies of Russia and the West who invented nuclear deterrence, are largely impervious to the temporal consequential logic upon which it is based.

The links between fundamentalist theory and nuclear destruction are becoming increasingly evident[1] to those in religious studies who have observed modern fundamentalism. Amongst North American fundamentalists there appears to be a framework of ideas which links confrontation between Russia and the West in the Middle East, the final destruction of Israel, nuclear holocaust, the heavenly 'rapture' of born-again Christians and the return of Christ. The exact chronological order of these events may vary from one fundamentalist group to another, yet their association together seems widespread. They may even be associated in the minds of some of those with access to nuclear weapons.

It will be the final irony if a largely secular intelligentsia discovers too late that religious studies should have been a part of their education. They have already had one warning. As has been pointed out earlier,[2] few predicted the possibility that Shi'ite fundamentalism could actually reverse the supposedly immutable process of secularization in Iran. The attractions of Western capitalism, consumerism and permissiveness, were thought to be so self-evident, that few realized that religious fundamentalism could actually reverse them. Yet it did. Likewise the horrors of nuclear warfare are so self-evident to nuclear strategists and the politicians who rely upon them, that it becomes quite unthinkable that anyone could ever use them. Religious fundamentalists may again prove them disastrously wrong. They still have powers long forgotten by a secular intelligentsia.

This chapter will examine some of the social and psychological structures undergirding these powers. Within the context of impending nuclear catastrophe, learning to identify these structures may be more important than is sometimes realized. Ignoring them might prove literally disastrous. It is the theory of cognitive dissonance which provides one of the most elegant and influential socio-psychological accounts of sectarian or fundamentalist reactions to impending catastrophe.

First this theory will be set out as it appears in the seminal book of 1956, *When Prophecy Fails*,[3] written jointly by Leon Festinger, Henry Riecken and Stanley Schachter. Then the chapter will briefly indicate some of the ways that this theory is playing an increasingly influential role in theology and religious studies. Thirdly it will face three of the recurring criticisms that theologians and biblical specialists make of the theory and its uses, based upon fears of reductionism, anachronistic use of modern-world theories, and the availability of sufficient social evidence relating to ancient communities. I will argue that all three fears are exaggerated. However, fourthly, a rather unexpected and damning criticism of my own will be offered: a careful examination of *When Prophecy Fails* reveals awkward questions about the accuracy and even veracity of its research. In offering this criticism I realize that I am challenging the very grounds of a theory which seems firmly established in socio-psychological orthodoxy. Finally, I will try to draw out from this discussion some of the key insights that a theologian might offer as remaining constant in our understanding of religious responses to impending disaster.

I

Despite its rather awesome name, cognitive dissonance theory has as at its centre a very straightforward premise, namely that someone with strong convictions is hard to change. On the opening page of *When Prophecy Fails* the authors extend this premise as follows:

> Suppose an individual believes something with his whole heart; suppose further that he has a commitment to this belief, that he has taken irrevocable actions because of it; finally, suppose that he is presented with evidence, unequivocal and undeniable evidence, that his belief is wrong: what will happen? The individual will frequently emerge, not only unshaken, but even more convinced of the truth of his beliefs than ever before. Indeed, he may even show a new fervour about convincing and converting other people to his view.[4]

So, for individuals experiencing the dissonance caused by their beliefs being confronted with falsifying evidence, abandonment of these beliefs may be their logical response, but, in practice, it is not their only response. Some individuals respond to such dissonance by becoming even more aggressively evangelical. Indeed, it is not difficult to observe that many of us become most dogmatic about those values and beliefs that guide us, but for which we have the least objective evidence. Academics may be almost as prone to this tendency as religious fundamentalists. Theologians have long argued that secularism and positivism can be dogmatic, unveri-fiable, and curiously evangelistic. Cognitive dissonance theory, however, is making a more specific claim than that. It is concerned with situations which confront groups holding strong convictions with clear and undeniable disproof of these convictions. Even when this happens, the theory maintains, such groups may paradoxically respond with increased evangelistic fervour. In these circumstances proselytism may be less a sign of religious conviction than an attempt to overcome dissonance.

For this to happen five conditions are necessary:

1. A belief must be held with deep conviction and it must have some relevance to action, that is, to what the believer does or how he behaves.

2. The person holding the belief must have committed himself to it; that is, for the sake of his belief, he must have taken some important action that is difficult to undo . . .

3. The belief must be sufficiently specific and sufficiently concerned with the real world so that events may unequivocally refute the belief.

4. Such undeniable disconfirmatory evidence must occur and must be recognized by the individual holding the belief . . .

5. The individual believer must have social support.[5]

The ideal people to fit the theory would have deep and committed beliefs that had led them both to give up their jobs to join a community of fellow believers and to make specific predictions about the fate of the world. They would then be confronted with evidence which disproved these predictions. They would acknowledge this evidence. Yet, so the theory claims, they could be expected to respond with a heightened sense of evangelism and a renewed attempt to proselytize others.

All five elements are important. They do not specifically depend upon religious convictions or religious groups or communities. Political groups of the far right or of the far left could well fulfil the requirements, provided that they make specific and refutable claims which they subsequently know to have been refuted. Social support is crucial. It is precisely the mutual support of fellow believers which allows individuals to persist with convictions even when they really know that they have been refuted. Together individuals in deviant groups can support each other and protect themselves from outside scepticism. The twist in the tail of cognitive dissonance theory is that they can be expected to do this by actually increasing their attempts to convert outside sceptics. It can even be the case that previously non-evangelistic groups become aggressively evangelistic as a result of an experience of dissonance and disconfirmation.

The first thirty pages of *When Prophecy Fails* set out the theory, illustrating it with a number of historical examples. The authors are aware that these examples lack the detailed empirical information which would be needed to demonstrate the theory. This they supply through an extended and very remarkable case-study that occupies the rest of the book. Having postulated the theory they noticed a news item in the Lake City *Herald* in late September (the year is not specified) under the dramatic headline: *Prophecy From Planet. Clarion Call To City: Flee That Flood. It'll Swamp Us On Dec. 21, Outer Space Tells Suburbanite*. The item read as follows:

> Lake City will be destroyed by a flood from Great Lake just before dawn, Dec. 21, according to a suburban housewife. Mrs Marian Keech, of 847 West School street, says the prophecy is not her own. It is the purport of many messages she has received by automatic writing, she says . . . The messages, according to Mrs Keech, are sent to her by superior beings from a planet called 'Clarion'. These beings have been visiting the earth, she says, in what we call flying saucers. During their visits, she says, they have observed fault lines in the earth's crust that foretoken the deluge. Mrs Keech reports she was told the flood will spread to form an island sea stretching from the Arctic Circle to the Gulf of Mexico. At the same time, she says, a cataclysm will submerge the West Coast from Seattle, Wash., to Chile in South America.[6]

It was at once clear to the authors that this might supply the crucial empirical test that was necessary to establish their theory. A specific and dated prediction had been made which was amenable to falsification. If there was a group of individuals jointly committed to this prediction it could be studied over the next three months. And if the theory of cognitive dissonance was to be verified, increased proselytism should be the reaction of the group after December 21st. This, indeed, is exactly what the authors and their five research assistants observed.

They visited Mrs Keech and quickly established that she had a long association with religious cults, such as Dianetics (which later became Scientology), as well as with flying saucer groups. She received her messages (through her automatic writing) from a variety of spiritual beings from the planets Clarion and Cerus. Chief amongst these was Sananda, whom she gradually came to see as the contemporary identity of Jesus. At first the messages offered general warnings about impending catastrophe, some of which were connected with nuclear warfare and others with natural disasters. Gradually they became more specific, culminating with the actual date of the future catastrophe reported in the news item. The authors also established that a group of believers was beginning to gather around Mrs Keech. A campus physician, Dr Armstrong and his wife, were particularly active. It was Dr Armstrong who had informed the newspaper and had written the release and it was he who formed interested students into a group called the Seekers.

Having concluded that all the constituents necessary for their social experiment were present, the authors hurriedly formed a research team and trained student researchers to investigate and become actively involved in the group surrounding Mrs Keech. They invented identities for the students and even gave them stories of cultic experiences to make them acceptable to the group. Then they waited to see what would happen when the inevitable disconfirmation occurred on December 21st. The long anecdotal account that they give of the group's behaviour leading up to and immediately after this date occupies almost half of the book. It is a very remarkable account and at every point it reinforces the theory that the empirical refutation of the prediction, although at first discouraging to individuals, soon led to vigorous proselytism. And this in a group which had previously been very reluctant to engage in active evangelism.

As the impending disaster drew near the group became increasingly querulous. There was a degree of rivalry between Mrs Keech mediating messages from Sananda and another woman claiming to mediate messages from the Creator himself. At one point in this competitive revelation the second woman predicted that Mr Keech (not a believer) would die that night and be resurrected. Disconfirmation of this prediction led to a spiritual re-interpretation. Mr Keech had died and risen again, but not in ways that could be observed directly by the group. In the few days and hours leading up to December 21st, Mrs Keech, in turn, made a series of predictions that a flying saucer would arrive to collect members of the group and save them from the impending disaster. Each deadline passed with considerable soul-searching, but eventually with a fresh interpretation (e.g. it had just been a test of faith) and then a new prediction.

At last the fateful day came and passed. The researchers in the group pressed the others for their reactions. Certain individuals were indeed disillusioned and left, never to return. However, most stayed and re-interpreted their experience. The world had been granted a reprieve. Extra time was being allowed for evangelization. A new researcher who joined the group only after the date was treated as a visitor from one of the planets. So they had come after all! Five strangers who came to the house were also regarded as ethereal visitors. Members of the group differed radically from each other about these appearances. The re-interpretations varied.

What united the group was their determination to carry on. Previously quiescent members (e.g. the Armstrong daughter) became strong in the faith and determined to tell all who would listen about its veracity. Media attention reached a crescendo on the day of prediction. Yet, whereas previously members of the group had been very reluctant to talk to such a sceptical audience, now they used every means open to them to publicize their faith. In short, disconfirmation led to a new found proselytism.

The media attention also attracted the attention of the police. Neighbours and parents had strongly protested. Soon into the New Year the group was disbanded. However, the Armstrongs remained believers. Having lost his medical post he became a touring evangelist. Mrs Keech continued her activities elsewhere and other members of the group also found new missionary zeal. In contrast, the Seekers, who, as students, had almost entirely gone home for the Christmas vacation, experienced the most disillusionment. For the authors of *When Prophecy Fails* this was a clear indication of the need for an active supporting group. It was this that sustained all but a very few of those intimately involved in the central group. Together they could overcome the obvious dissonance caused by the failure of the prediction of impending disaster to materialize. And together they could re-interpret their experience, unwittingly encouraging each other to overcome dissonance with vigorous proselytism.

The case-study was regarded as a dramatic proof of the theory of cognitive dissonance. The authors had been able to specify its required conditions and their likely outcome. They had been able to unmask the social mechanisms that such deviant groups use to sustain dissonant beliefs. And in the process they had shown how educated, if somewhat eccentric, individuals can maintain deviant beliefs and even re-invigorate them in the face of empirical falsification. All of this is highly relevant to understanding how modern fundamentalists can maintain convictions that are at odds with the cultural pluralism that surrounds them.

II

When Prophecy Fails has been an immensely influential book. Festinger, this time writing on his own, followed it immediately with *A Theory of Cognitive Dissonance*[7] (it is from this book that the theory properly-speaking derives its name) and for some years the *Journal of Abnormal and Social Psychology* carried many articles on it. It has now passed into social psychology and the sociology of religion as an accepted orthodoxy. For an analysis of sects, such as the Jehovah's Witness Movement, which make specific and refutable predictions of impending catastrophe, it has been widely accepted as a convincing and fruitful theory. It has been particularly influential in linking the aggressive proselytism of such sects with the fragility created by their specific predictions.

Gradually it has also come to occupy a role in biblical studies. There can be little doubt, as I will argue further in chapter 7, that the social sciences will play an increasing role in these studies.[8] There has been a particularly sharp increase in sociological accounts of the New Testament. This does now seem to be one of the more exciting areas of New Testament scholarship since it offers fresh insights into a discipline that can sometimes become repetitive and circular. One of the ways that disciplines gain a new lease of life and fresh vigour in the scholarly world is when a different method or new empirical data are brought into it. Cognitive dissonance theory offers both a fresh method and new comparative data. It is not difficult to see why it has attracted biblical scholars such as Robert Carroll or John Gager.

Robert Carroll's *When Prophecy Failed*,[9] despite its rather dramatic title, makes very judicious use of cognitive dissonance theory. He is aware that the Old Testament material which is most amenable to the theory – Isaiah, Jeremiah and the post-exilic prophets – never fully satisfies all five of the conditions already outlined. There are strong predictions of impending disaster in these prophetic writings and it is these that encourage Carroll to use cognitive dissonance theory. Yet it is difficult to find unequivocal predictions which were both falsified and known to have been falsified by the prophets themselves. Carroll concludes modestly:

> The main thrust of my argument for the existence of response to dissonance in the prophetic traditions is the amount of *re*interpreted material in those traditions. The accumulated growth of the prophetic traditions incorporated numerous responses to problems of failure and seriously modified motifs that had become obsolete. Changes in social and political circumstances destroyed the realization of the hope for a Davidic king but interpretative elements within prophecy transformed the hope into one of the city as the throne for the *divine* king (e.g. Jer. 3.17; cf. Isa. 28.5; 33.17, 21; Ezek. 48.35).[10]

In a supporting article Carroll shows that he is well aware of the implications, and the difficulties, of cognitive dissonance being applied additionally to the New Testament. At one point he even envisages an ambitious programme analysing 'text plus its interpretation within various communities embracing it as holy scripture or authoritative writ' and using the theory for this analysis. He is aware that 'this means the material available for research is increased to include the fields of biblical exegesis and its history, historical theology and the multiple forms of sects deriving their existence from discrete interpretations of the Bible'.[11] However, in the end, he finds such a programme too daunting.

Nonetheless other theologians have continued to move in this direction. Once theology is viewed as a social system – that is as a socially and culturally relative attempt to interpret our abiding relationship to God – then the relevance of such a programme becomes obvious. But such an understanding of theology will have to wait until the final chapter.

The most impressive attempt to apply cognitive dissonance theory to the New Testament is perhaps to be found in John Gager's *Kingdom and Community*.[12] First published in 1975, this little book is remarkable for its methodological sophistication. Apart from the more eclectic Wayne Meeks,[13] few other scholars have matched his ability to apply sociological theory to New Testament material. If Norman Gottwald is to be recognized as the leading Old Testament sociologist,[14] then Gager must be amongst the leading New Testament sociologists. Both are well aware of the dangers of applying social models and paradigms to biblical material, yet both insist that if they are applied with care they can allow us 'to see old facts in a new light'.[15]

The aim of *Kingdom and Community* is to study the way a social world is constructed and maintained in early Christianity: 'to explore . . . the relationship between religion and social status, the enthusiastic character of the earliest Christian communities, their gradual transformation into a formidable religious and social institution, and the emergence of Christianity as the dominant religion of the later Roman Empire'.[16] Cognitive dissonance becomes a central theory in this exploration. Gager argues that it is not hermeneutics but proselytism that is the major outcome of dissonance within earliest Christianity. He identifies two catastrophes that faced the earliest Christians, the death of Jesus and the expectation of the Kingdom of God. In the responses to both he detects signs of dissonance leading to increased proselytism. He does not claim that the theory will account for *all* forms of early missionary activity. Like others,[17] he maintains that the theory needs some supplementation (e.g. that public ridicule at the time of disconfirmation is an important factor). Nonetheless, it is the basic theory developed in *When Prophecy Fails* that provides a central plank in his account of the growth of earliest Christianity.

III

Some theologians may feel uneasy about using cognitive dissonance theory as a way of understanding how religious groups cope with impending catastrophe. It is one thing to apply it to a marginal flying saucer cult, but it is quite another to use it as a means of understanding the missionary zeal of early Christianity. Theologians may be happy to watch sociologists using such theories on groups that they regard as marginal and frankly deluded. They may be less than happy to use sociology in this way to understand Christian origins. Three objections, in particular, are frequently encountered – reductionism, anachronism, and evidence.[18]

At first sight there does appear to be a strong reductionist element in sociological accounts of religious beliefs. Some sociologists, with religious convictions themselves, have even argued that the sociology of religion is essentially a sociology of error.[19] Cognitive dissonance theory would seem to be no exception. The case-study in *When Prophecy Fails* derives much of its force from the fact that we know that the beliefs and predictions of the group are absurd. The research workers did not have to wait until December 21st to discover whether or not the predictions of impending catastrophe would materialize. On the contrary, they picked the group because they knew its predictions would be falsified and they wanted to observe the reactions of the group members when they found this out for themselves. Like other functionalists, particularly those following Durkheim in *The Elementary of the Religious Life* who presume they are examining 'primitive' mentalities, the authors have a strong (and for some quite fatal)[20] tendency towards tautology in their method.

Again, applying theories derived from data from twentieth-century urban society to a first-century rural or semi-urban community does appear to be anachronistic. For example, modern sociology makes presumptions about social class which are highly dependent upon post-industrial observations. It is far from clear that they apply to ancient communities. The case-study in *When Prophecy Fails* relates to a community that is not just post-industrial and urban, but also has fantasies derived from twentieth-century science fiction. Like scientology, it produces a peculiarly post-scientific syncretism of religious symbols and extra-terrestrial accretions, quite beyond the wildest dreams of the earliest Christians.

Thirdly, there is the question of evidence. Modern sociology depends upon an array of scientific procedures – ethnographic statistics, questionnaire-surveys, structured field observations, etc. – none of which are available to those applying sociology to ancient communities. The authors of *When Prophecy Fails* are themselves aware of this deficiency and it is for this reason that they finally decide that evidence about earliest Christianity is insufficient for their theory. Gager and others seem to ignore this warning.

In fact they do not. The more sophisticated exponents of biblical sociology – such as Gottwald and Gager – spend a considerable amount of time discussing these objections. They are well aware of the suspicion of reductionism. Yet they are also aware of the distinction between 'explaining something' and 'explaining something away'. There have been versions of sociological imperialism which have seemed oblivious to this distinction. However, more mature sociology soon realized that reductionism is self-defeating. Reductionists themselves can soon be reduced by their own canons. All knowledge, even scientific knowledge, can be viewed in social terms, including the knowledge offered by the sociology of knowledge. Origins and validity are distinct. So, if someone tells me that I am a theologian because I had a strong attachment to my clerical grandfather, they are not actually telling me anything about the validity of my views as a theologian. Validity must be decided on other grounds. Similarly, even if a connection is made between dissonance and the proselytism of early Christians, we still must decide on other grounds about the latter's validity. In any case, Gager is emphatic that cognitive dissonance theory does not account for all early Christian missionary activity.

Again, the more sophisticated biblical sociologists are well aware of the dangers of anachronism and insufficient evidence. They would surely agree that there *is* insufficient evidence to establish a theory of cognitive disonnance from early Christianity. The authors of *When Prophecy Fails* were correct when they realized that they could not properly establish their theory on such a basis. Yet, once the theory is established, it is quite a different matter. Sociology is in fact committed to the idea that there are regularities in human social behaviour. It does attempt to establish theories from specific situations which can then be applied to other situations. Of course it is more risky doing this diachronically – across periods of time – and of course the scholar must be cautious when there is also a paucity of empirical evidence. Yet biblical scholars perennially face these difficulties. There is nothing very unusual for them about applying theories which have been developed in the twentieth century to their own subject matter. And they are well used to being tentative when handling evidence that lacks outside corroboration.

Gottwald argues at length[21] that sociological method does not just bring a fresh perspective to biblical studies, it also brings a spur to further research. He sets out in detail the sort of ethnographic, archaeological and comparative research that could be done on ancient communities once sociological questions are raised. This will not eliminate the need for speculation and imaginative application of theory. How could it ever in biblical studies? It is an important part of what makes such studies academically exciting. Yet it might provide a firmer basis than is currently available. Established sociological theories could then be applied back to biblical communities with greater confidence.

IV

But an important question remains. Is cognitive dissonance really an established theory? This question may seem strange since it has already been shown that the theory is widely accepted in socio-psychological orthodoxy. It has been supplemented in a number of ways, but its position seems secure. Further, it has evidently become established in biblical studies and I have argued that its theological critics are not finally persuasive. Perhaps the question ought properly to be, should cognitive dissonance be accepted as an established theory?

The theory itself has been widely discussed. However the veracity of the case-study that was used to establish it has received little attention. For most theologians truthfulness is a prerequisite, but the case-study in *When Prophecy Fails* is built upon deceit. The research workers were taught to lie systematically in order to gain entry into the group, to adopt fabricated preternatural experiences to gain the confidence of the group leaders, and to continue to lie for some three months whilst appearing to be committed members of the group. This systematic and remarkably skilful deceit contrasts sharply with the high ethical standards set by the mentor of most corresponding British research, Bryan Wilson.[22] For him it is essential that research workers make their sociological intentions unambiguously clear to a group at the outset.

It is not simply professionalism which is at stake here, although surely for most ethical academics that *is* important. Rather it is trustworthiness. If people admit to deceit in their methods, how can we trust their findings? Suspicions are raised. A careful analysis of the case-study in question does raise some curious dissonances. In the final paragraph the authors admit that, 'our data, in places, are less complete than we would like, our influence on the group somewhat greater than we would like'. Nevertheless, they insist that, 'we were able, however, to collect enough information to tell a coherent story and, fortunately, the effects of disconfirmation were striking enough to provide for firm conclusions'.[23]

The word 'story' in this sentence is not the only dissonant note in the book. At times there is almost an element of spoof about parts of it. They date their preface December 21st: they depict members of the group hurriedly cutting out the zips from their trousers or clasps from their bras in case the metal should interfere with the expected flying saucer: a telephone call from a 'Captain Video' is taken seriously by members of the group. There is even a Passion Narrative structure to the 'story' presented in the case-study. There are believers and the occasional doubting disciple: there is the death and resurrection of a man: there is a physician evangelist: there are varying and conflicting accounts of extra-terrestrial appearances after December 21st: and there is finally a proselytizing diaspora.

Again, we are asked to believe that the group simply accepted the student research workers as members. There is no indication given at any point over the three months that even the educated members of the group were suspicious. And this was despite the hurried training given to the research workers and despite the prolonged intimacy of the group itself. The research workers together represented about a third of the membership of the central group. Yet their real purpose apparently remained hidden to the genuine group members throughout the time in question. Their clandestine activities – such as making transcripts of entire telephone calls – were seemingly undetected.

An indication that something is desperately wrong emerges from a detailed comparison of the case-study with the fictionalized version of it that appears in Alison Lurie's *Imaginary Friends*.[24] The skilled novelist instructively changes those very elements of un-detected, prolonged deceit by five partially trained students that seem so incredible in the case-study itself. In *Imaginary Friends* it is two, not five, sociologists who penetrate the flying saucer group, and they are both fully-trained academics (one a full professor with considerable experience). Further, the more junior academic has real scruples about deceiving the group and, very early, the cover of both is blown. They then admit to the group that they are sociologists, but insist that they are still interested. And they remain within the group only on that basis.

It is clear that *Imaginary Friends* is based upon *When Prophecy Fails*. Not only do some of the characters and much of the story correspond, but so does the early description of the senior sociologist's theory:

> McMann's basic hypothesis was that a certain minimum amount of opposition would actually be good for such a group. For one thing, up to a point the energy which the members would have to expend answering the doubts, or combating the opposition, would unite them and involve them as individuals more deeply. Even a disproof from the natural order (as, for example, the non-appearance of men from outer space) would not necessarily be fatal. His theory was a disconfirmation of this sort would not really weaken a well-established group, as long as the members faced it together. They would simply rationalize what had happened, and alter their convictions just as much as was necessary to preserve the belief system and the group – both of which probably existed for non-ideological reasons anyway, and filled important social needs.[25]

Alison Lurie finally turns the story into farce. The professor of sociology apparently becomes one of the group's most ardent believers and himself an object of belief. The parody of the expense of sociology is obvious. But perhaps the original case-study deserves such parody.

Of course the authors of *When Prophecy Fails* to admit to an 'influence on the group somewhat greater than we would like'. This admission is remarkable only for its understatement. At the key moment of disconfirmation they report that the research workers acted as follows:

> During this break, which lasted for about half an hour, everyone in the group was reluctant to talk about the failure of the midnight prediction – everyone, that is, except the five observers who wanted to talk about it very much. They kept asking the others in the house such questions as 'What do you think happened to the man who was supposed to come at midnight?' 'Why didn't he come?' 'What did the miracle have to do with his not coming?' 'Will the saucer still pick us up?' and so on.[26]

Not only did this probing raise no suspicions, but it also

apparently played no significant part in shaping the 'striking' reaction of the group to disconfirmation. The research workers were fortunate indeed. Those who are more cautious might have supposed that discreet silence would have been less likely to taint the results and to risk detection.

The more the case-study is inspected the less capable it seems of bearing the weight of the theory. It occupies a key role in *When Prophecy Fails*. Much of the book is devoted to it and it is clearly intended to establish cognitive dissonance theory on a firm basis. Yet those who have been so influenced by it seem to have given most of their attention to the theory itself and failed to subject the case-study to rigorous scrutiny. Much of the case-study is of course beyond scrutiny. The authors claim that they deliberately changed all the names and places within it 'to protect the actual people involved in the movement from the curiosity of an unsympathetic reader'.[27] Further, like the work of Sir Cyril Birt on separately reared identical twins, the subject matter of the case-study (a tightly circumscribed but inspectable group making public and refutable predictions) is rare and difficult to replicate. Yet the parts of the case-study that are open to critical scrutiny stretch credulity very considerably.

V

What can be rescued from cognitive dissonance theory in attempting to understand how fundamentalist groups cope with impending catastrophe? Not the specific link between dissonance and proselytism. It is this link which is the most distinctive part of the theory and for which the case-study is most needed. And it is this link which has been subject to most revision amongst socio-psychologists. However, if we cannot presume that the link is established in *When Prophecy Fails*, we need not then attempt to revise it to fit awkward counter-examples. So the stimulating use that Gager makes of this distinctive part of the theory must also be questioned.

Other parts of the theory are not so vulnerable, since they are largely dependent upon a wide variety of sociological observations of deviant groups. Studies in the sociology of deviance (the term is used to depict dissent from conformity, not of course moral perversity) well indicate how groups can foster, reinforce and spread convictions that are at odds with society at large. In this respect minority fundamentalist groups have much in common with many other deviant political or youth groups. The transcendental features of religious groups make them particularly impervious to outside scepticism. If a sect (such as the Exclusive Brethren or the

Jehovah's Witnesses) builds tight membership barriers against
society at large, it can successfully maintain and foster socially
deviant beliefs. Self-contained groups can develop their own
plausibility structures and protect themselves, if that is necessary,
from prevailing 'commonsense'. That much, at least, does seem to
be established.

For a theologian that perhaps is sufficient. Critical theology offers
a double perspective on the immediate issue of coping with
impending nuclear catastrophe. It offers warnings both to secularists and to religious fundamentalists. To secularists it offers timely
warnings about the fundamentalists. The latter's powers are not to
be underestimated and their apocalyptic visions are to be feared if
they gain access to political power. Secular disdain has been
remarkably ineffective in tempering Shi'ite fundamentalism and
secular analysis, as has been seen, largely failed to foresee its
resurgence. Theology offers a quite different vision of the world
from secularism. It sees the world as created rather than fortuitous
and as the gift of a loving God. *Sub specie aeternitatis* nuclear
catastrophe is not simply a human catastrophe but a catastrophe
that involves the created order. The theologian offers an additional
dimension of seriousness to the secularist. Life is not ours to
replicate or destroy at will, but a gift requiring gratitude and
responsibility.

Critical theology also offers warnings to religious fundamentalists. They distort religious beliefs by hypostasizing relative doctrines. If theology is indeed seen as a social system, then it is only
our relationship to God, not the verbal expressions of this
relationship, that is constant. I will argue in chapter 7 that modern
theology is increasingly aware of the plurality of both Christian and
world religious beliefs. As faculties of theology become increasingly
ecumenical, the varied and rich resources of Christianity become
ever more apparent. Fundamentalists seek to overcome this
plurality by claiming a monopoly of truth for their own convictions.
Such claims may be comparatively harmless if they are made by the
politically marginal. However they become potentially catastrophic
if they belong to those with access to nuclear weapons.

Bruce Malina suggests an alternative understanding of cognitive
dissonance which perhaps makes better *theological* sense of a
fundamentalist response to impending catastrophe. He suggests
that dissonance, or some degree of normative inconsistency, is a
feature of much of everyday life and religious consciousness. It is
the fundamentalist who seeks to reduce this dissonance by insisting

upon an unambiguous doctrinal or ethical perspective. Reversing Gager, Malina even argues that 'a model of dissonance and ambivalence . . . might explain why earliest Christianity did in fact avoid extremism and survive, while not a few factions from the same period ended in destruction'.[28]

When Prophecy Fails presumes that dissonance is associated with fragility in marginal groups. Malina agrees rather with those who have argued that fragility is not necessarily a feature of unconventional or fundamentalist beliefs at all. Leaving aside the world of specific and refutable predictions, a more critical theological perspective might suggest that religious faith surely is elusive and at times dissonant. A somewhat modified version of cognitive dissonance theory offers a sociological account of how fundamentalist groups may 'successfully' bypass relativism. However, for the critical theologian, they achieve this 'success' only by ignoring the cultural relativism that is present even within the earliest phases of Christianity itself. The next three chapters will illustrate how a sociological approach to the churches serves to highlight this internal cultural relativism and the dysfunctionality of competing convictions.

PART TWO

Churches and Competing Convictions

---

4 · Understanding Church Decline

Amongst sociologists of religion there is a strong presumption that active co-operation between churches contributes to their mutual decline. Ecumenism, however desirable it might seem to theologians or church leaders, is often thought to weaken and to secularize religious convictions and to contribute to the demise of religious institutions.[1] On this theory, radically competing churches are more likely than ecumenically-minded denominations to preach their convictions with fervour and to evangelize the general population. Ecumenical denominations, in contrast, are less convinced about the uniqueness of their own convictions and are correspondingly less motivated to proselytize.

The various forms of fundamentalism and sectarianism studied in the last two chapters might be thought to confirm this interpretation. The scriptural absolutism that characterizes fundamentalism in any form is indeed absolutist. Fundamentalists are typically dogmatic and uncompromising in their convictions. Confronted with others holding competing absolutist convictions, they are not given to compromise. Far from it, their counter-cultural habits incline them to attack. They are already at considerable odds with modernity and are scarcely likely to adopt a *laissez-faire* attitude towards rival convictions. Their very ideological strength resides in their own absolutist convictions and it may be this that makes them such a potent and troublesome force in a more pluralistic world.

If Malina's understanding of cognitive dissonance within sectarianism is adopted, then it would seem that certitude and absolutism are the means through which otherwise fragile religious groups maintain their unity and fervour. The single-minded convictions of sectarian groups differentiate them from society at large (which is only too well aware of the essential ambiguity of life) and give them a common purpose in seeking to change society. But churches are themselves caught up in ambiguity and, although they might more adequately represent society, they are at the same time distinctly less able to challenge and change that society. For this reason, over time churches inevitably secularize and decline. Stark and Bainbridge have argued at length[2] that secularization consists of a long-term process of church decline punctuated by occasional sharp sectarian reversals. Using Richard Niebuhr's thesis[3] that sects either die or soon turn into denominations, they maintain that it is sects which reverse secularization, but that it is denominations which predominate in history and which carry the seeds of secularization. The latter irresistibly compromise with society, provoking occasional sectarian reversals but more usually diluting their distinctively religious convictions.

Christine King's remarkable study of the Jehovah's Witnesses' response to Nazism well illustrates this pattern of fundamentalism.[4] She contrasts the collaborationist responses of many churches and some sects in Germany towards the Nazis with the absolutist response of the Witnesses. Mormons, she suggests, could successfully co-exist with ideological Nazis, since their racial views and their active pursuit of details of their (aryan) ancestors were often well received by Nazis. The New Apostolic Church flew the Swastika flag over its church buildings and held church parades for party members in uniform. And Adventists changed references to 'the sabbath' to 'the rest-day' and removed terms such as 'Zion' from their liturgy.

Jehovah's Witnesses, in contrast, were implacable opponents of the Nazi regime. In 1934 they declared that, 'We would delight to dwell in peace and good will to all men as we have opportunity, but since your government and its officers continue in your attempt to force us to disobey the highest law of the universe, we are compelled to now give you notice that we will, by His grace, obey Jehovah-God and fully trust Him to deliver us from all oppression and oppressors.'[5] As a result, by 1945 King estimates that of the 20,000 Witnesses in Germany back in 1933, 10,000 were in prison and 4,000–5,000 had been executed. Faced with an absolutist and totalitarian regime, the Witnesses reacted as an absolutist counter-culture and were persecuted accordingly.

King argues that there are many points of similarity between the ideological positions of the Witnesses and the Nazis:

This was a conflict between two systems so similar in their totalitarian claims, that Germany would not contain them both. Both were new, both presented total world views and an authoritarian world system; both were millenarian, fundamentalist, Messianic, anti-intellectual; both demanded fanatical devotion from their followers; both were uncompromising. Between these two rival claimants on loyalty, the fight was bitter, even more so, since the physically stronger Nazis were in many ways less sure, less rooted in the firmness of their own conviction, less certain of the survival of their 1,000 year Reich. Witnesses did not doubt their own roots, for their faith had been evident since the time of Abel.[6]

From a strictly sociological perspective, the inevitable compromises of ecumenism seem more akin to the responses of the collaborationist churches and sects within Nazi Germany than to the absolutist counter-cultural response of the Jehovah's Witnesses. It might be argued that the long-term survival of the Witnesses, and their attractiveness to minorities in many parts of the world, is a product of their uncompromising convictions. Even within Britain they have successfully maintained their predominantly working-class, sectarian roots throughout this century.

Once again the theologian may have considerable cause for unease with this sociological interpretation. It is difficult to be theologically sympathetic with a sect as scripturally absolutist, exclusivist and idiosyncratic as that of the Jehovah's Witnesses. Whilst applauding the sect's moral courage in the face of Nazi totalitarianism (and more recent forms of totalitarianism in some Communist and Third World countries), few may feel inclined to applaud the theology that underlies it. Yet Christine King's evidence is hardly comfortable for the theologian, especially for the ecumenical theologian.

However, it is possible that this sociological analysis is too simplistic. Certainly it is characteristically based upon generalized data rather than upon the detailed study of churches. If sociologists have given considerable attention to sects and to new religious movements over the last twenty years, they have seldom studied churches or denominations with the same level of scholarship. Instead, they have tended to make sweeping generalizations about such phenomena as church decline. In this section I hope to offer an alternative approach relying instead upon very detailed empirical study. I will argue as a result that it offers a radical challenge to the prevailing sociological orthodoxies that I have just outlined. This research is a part of my ongoing research project on church decline in the North East of England and at several points I will indicate briefly where it is likely to lead next. It is still tentative and its results (especially on urban church decline) are only provisional. Yet it may already throw fresh light on the social function of competing convictions within churches.

I

The extent to which sociologists, even whilst engaged on the detailed study of sects and new religious movements, rely instead upon generalized data for churches, is most obvious in the secularization debate. The seminal work of Bryan Wilson typifies this. His own contribution to the study of small-scale religious movements is inestimable. By pioneering specific and local studies of these movements he has inspired a whole generation of sociologists of religion. Yet his discussions of secularization tend to be highly generalized, relying upon national rather than local data. An analysis of his Riddell Memorial Lectures,[7] given at the University of Newcastle upon Tyne in December 1974, highlights this contrast.

If Wilson's analysis in these lectures of present-day secularization is correct then there is little to understand about church decline. The latter is part of a broad process of secularization in which 'religious commitment and the belief in the power of the supernatural are declining in the modern world'.[8] The modern world is becoming irresistibly secular. It is scientific, rationalistic and bureaucratic procedures that dominate our social experience, not religious or magical modes of thought. As a result religious institutions will become increasingly epiphenomenal. Their gradual demise is inevitable. Only religious sects, which have built tight barriers against a hostile world, can expect to survive, isolated and socially marginal. Churches will continue to vanish.

Of course it would still be possible to analyse church decline. There may be local variations in the speed of this decline and Wilson is well aware of temporary charismatic revivals and sectarian resurgences even in the West. However he does not believe that these are anything other than temporary pauses in an overall process of secularization. This process ultimately carries all before it. He does not applaud this – indeed he believes that the loss of community that it incurs can be painful – he merely argues that it is a social reality.

This social reality renders any major attempt to understand church decline in terms other than those of secularization largely irrelevant. It also makes nonsense of any theologically inspired attempt to find ways of actually reversing church decline. It might be better for applied theologians with a sociological bent to work out strategies for churches to accept their inevitable demise, rather than pretending that they can survive, let alone thrive, long-term in the modern world.

For Wilson secularization is evident in changes in religious beliefs, attitudes, behaviour and institutions. Church decline is only a part of this process. Wilson argues as follows:

> All the evidence from our own times suggests that, at least in the Western world, Christian faith is in serious decline. What is true of the institutions of the church appears also to be true of the belief and the practice of the majority of men. Religion, particularly in its traditional form, has become socially less and less significant. Most modern men, for most of their time, in most of their activities, are very little touched – if they are touched at all – by any direct religious intimations. Even those who count themselves as believers, who subscribe to the tenets of a church, and who attend services regularly, nevertheless operate in social space in which their beliefs about the supernatural are rendered in large part irrelevant.[9]

As a result of the long-term effects of secularization, religious faith of any description has become difficult for people in the modern world. It is not simply the superficial features of archaic forms of religion, anachronistic church practices or beliefs, that cause difficulty. Rather it is 'the irreconcilability of the suppositions of faith in the supernatural and its arbitrary unexplained authority, and the suppositions that underlie all other activities and operations in which modern men engage in their everyday lives'.[10] It would seem that for Wilson secularization has at its base cognitive incredulity in supernatural modes of thought and explanation. The loss of power and even moral authority by religious institutions, their gradual decline in active membership and adherence, and the social and numerical demise of their clergy all apparently stem from this incredulity. 'Statistics reveal social processes, but they do not expose the causes of contemporary change, nor do they intimate the type of tensions that currently exist within the churches.'[11] To understand these it is necessary to keep remembering that faith in the supernatural is incredible in the modern world. He is impressed (despite strong reservations about questionnaire surveys in general) with evidence from the early 1970s suggesting that less people believe in God or afterlife than in the 1960s. For instance, a Gallup Poll in 1968 showed that 54% of the people professed to believe in heaven, whereas in 1974 only 39% apparently believed in afterlife at all.[12]

Evidence about church decline is consonant with this. He points to the drop in Easter communicants in the Church of England from just under 10% of adults before the First World War to 5.6% in 1968: to a drop in the electoral roll of the Church of England from c. 3,700,000 in 1930 to c. 2,700,000 in 1968: a reduction in baptisms from more than 60% of all live births in 1956 to less than 50% in 1968. He also points to major losses of membership in the Baptists, Methodists and Congregationalists. 'Between 10% and 12% of the population of England and Wales attend a church on Sundays, but this figure is so high only because for Roman Catholics attendance is an obligation, but even among Catholics decline has occurred.'[13]

Had Wilson been giving these lectures today this statistical evidence would have been even more dramatic. The Free Churches in England have shown some of the sharpest declines in active membership and adherence. The Church of England and the Church of Scotland have both declined very considerably and even the Roman Catholic Church (the last major denomination in Britain to succumb) has declined steadily over the last two decades. In much of Europe the decline of the Catholic Church is now as pronounced as that evident in the national churches of England and Scotland.

Significantly, however, Wilson no longer tends to use church statistics in his most recent accounts of secularization.[14] This might be because of an odd asymmetry in his thought. It is true that in the West many churches are declining. But it is not true that all Western churches are declining. And in the West the United States of America is a very obvious example of a (perhaps the) modern, industrial, urban nation in which high levels of churchgoing persist. Wilson is aware of this, but accounts for it in divergent ways.

In *Religion in Secular Society*, written ten years earlier, Wilson acknowledged that the American churches had grown in membership very considerably since 1880. Then only 20% of the population had church membership. By 1926 27% had Protestant membership and 16% Catholic membership: by 1958 35% had Protestant membership and 22.8% Catholic membership. During the 1950s and 1960s 'about 45% of Americans attend church each week'.[15] Yet he was still convinced that the United States was a secular country. He argued that secularization had taken a different form there from that taken in Europe. Following Will Herberg he argued that in a land of diverse immigrant groups churches were an important way of expressing community identity. They performed a social rather than a religious function and were thus themselves a part of secularization.

In the Riddell Lectures he again stresses the social or community function of American churchgoing. However he now adds:

> But even in America the churches have experienced a decline from the late 1950s when a normal Sunday would see over 50% of the population in church: in 1972 only 40% were estimated to be in church on an ordinary Sunday. Attendances among Catholics diminished from 71% to 57% between 1964 and 1972.[16]

The changes between these two arguments are highly significant. The earlier account of secularization was aware of the oddity of using statistics of both membership decline (in Britain) and membership increase (in the USA) as consonant with, or even as evidence for, a process of secularization. Under this argument the British figures denoted the 'true' situation, whereas the American figures needed to be explained away (an argument of course that is dangerously reversible). Whereas in the later account evidence of membership decline could be found in both situations. In this second account the asymmetry is considerably reduced, but only by ignoring the longer-term American figures cited in the earlier account. Indeed, Protestant decline in the States can equally be interpreted as a return to the situation of the 1940s as a decline from the 1950s. And even by the mid-1970s there was already evidence of increase amongst conservative American churches to set alongside a decline in liberal and Catholic churches.

In the Riddell lectures Wilson's account of secularization is considerably more defensive than that in *Religion in Secular Society*. He responds at several points to sociological critics of secularization such as David Martin. He is clearly not persuaded by them, yet he is already aware that a model which was so dominant amongst sociologists of religion, political scientists, historians, religionists and even theologians in the 1960s, is under attack. In the 1980s this attack has continued and it is now Wilson who appears out of step.

This is very apparent in the distinguished collection edited in 1984 by Phillip Hammond, *The Sacred in a Secular Age*. As noted earlier, of all twenty-two contributors only Wilson presents an unmodified theory of secularization. In the introduction to the collection, sponsored by the Society for the Scientific Study of Religion,

Hammond points to three examples of 'the re-emergent sacred in a secular age'. There are the new religious movements which Wilson acknowledges in the Riddell lectures. But there are also the resurgent forms of conservative Protestantism in Europe and America. And there are also 'the undeniably religious element in the political situation found in Northern Ireland, Lebanon, Iran, India–Pakistan, Poland, and many places in Latin America. Religion is hardly moribund if these instances are taken seriously, but, to the degree they *are* taken seriously, they call for new thinking about the sacred.'[17]

It is unnecessary to rehearse again the literature from a number of disciplines which suggests that the theory that there is some ineluctable process of secularization is being increasingly questioned. It is, though, worth mentioning the collection edited by James Obelkevich with L. Roper and R. Samuel in 1987 for the Religion and Society History Workshop, entitled *Disciplines of Faith: Studies in Religion, Politics and Patriarchy* cited in chapter 2. The editors realize that their 'recognition of the power of religion as a shaping force of politics in the contemporary world . . . is uncomfortable for socialists who have traditionally anticipated the eventual triumph of reason over superstition, as it is for sociologists with their paradigms of secularization and rationalization, allegedly characteristic of the modern world'.[18]

In terms very similar to Hammond they argue:

> The power and extraordinary destiny of the Revolution in Iran; the bitterness of the war in Northern Ireland; the disturbing transformations effected by Jewish identity and consciousness in Israel; the role of the Catholic church in the solidarity movements in Poland; all show the inadequacy of such firmly held convictions as the commonplace that the modern world belongs to post-religious epoch . . . Even in the heart of the most advanced capitalist economy in the world, the United States of America, we are confronted by the recrudescence of the moral majority and the political mobilization of borne-again Christianity.[19]

Freed from this assumption that secularization is an ineluctable social process that gradually sweeps all but the most obdurate and marginal religious institutions before it, some younger social historians have taken a new interest in church decline. If church decline is not to be seen simply as part of secularization, how is it to be explained? The most promising answers are coming from scholars, such as James Obelkevich himself, Stephen Yeo, Jeffrey

Cox and Callum Brown, undertaking detailed and sustained local history research.[20] Amongst this research Jeffrey Cox's *The English Churches in a Secular Society: Lambeth, 1870–1930* is quite remarkable.

As the title of his work suggests Cox examines the social role and context of the churches in Lambeth, South London, at a crucial stage of transition. In 1870 all of the churches were relatively strong. They were visibly at the centre of social life in Lambeth. Most of the local population sent their children to Sunday School and a sizeable minority attended church. Most churches had strong community functions and were active in 'church work', or 'philanthropy' as Cox terms it. They provided important instruments of social esteem; with the Church of England being particularly attractive to the established middle classes and non-Conformist churches to artisans. The occasional offices that the churches provided were used by almost all within the community.

By 1930 the situation had changed dramatically. Churchgoing had declined very considerably. Local clergy no longer saw themselves as being at the centre of the social life of Lambeth. Sunday schools no longer attracted a preponderance of the local children. The philanthropic function of the churches had been largely handed over to, or expropriated by (according to one's perspective), secular authorities. And the latter offered numerous alternatives to the social esteem once offered by churches. Even the occasional offices (with the exception of funerals) ceased to be a point of contact between churches and the majority of the community.

Cox is conscious that many would simply explain this change in terms of secularization. But he is convinced that this is a mistake: 'It is difficult to overstate the extent to which the very best historians of Victorian religion are addicted to the language of inevitable and irreversible decline, decay, and failure, and explain that historical change with references to an underlying "process" of secularization'.[21] He argues that such historians tend to judge Victorian churches by the latter's own idealistic standards. The Victorian evangelicals in Lambeth (as elsewhere) often regarded anything less than the total conversion of society as failure, with the result that their own 'successes' appeared with historical hindsight to be 'failures' and then to be the product of an inevitable process of secularization.

Cox is perfectly well aware of the changes to our cosmology effected by scientific advances. Yet, perhaps as an American, he is also aware that science, technology, urbanization and modernization do not necessarily lead to church decline. They may even be associated (as they were in Lambeth in 1870) with a re-invigoration of institutional forms of religion:

> What I object to is the air of inevitability which results from wrapping all of these changes up into a package called 'the process of secularization' and using that package as an explanation of social change in the modern world. My objection to that concept is based upon an examination of the facts. The social changes involved in secularization do not invariably and inevitably lead to the decay of religious ideas and institutions. Furthermore, an appeal to an underlying process of secularization obscures a very interesting and ongoing adaption of religious forms to the modern world.[22]

Cox's case is so strong precisely because he engages in highly detailed local historical research, some of which offers alternative and more convincing explanations of church decline than secularization. Secularization appears as a very blunt instrument serving to obscure, as David Martin warned twenty years ago,[23] more subtle social processes. If secularization has to be used as an explanation it might be more illuminating if it was used only as a last resort. More mundane factors need to be thoroughly tested first.

Amongst these mundane factors Cox points to demographic and political changes that may have been instrumental in the sharp institutional decline of the Lambeth church between 1870 and 1930. The middle classes, which had been disproportionately represented amongst churchgoers and especially amongst church leaders, moved out into the affluent suburbs south of London. As a result Sunday Schools found difficulty in recruiting teachers (especially male teachers who had once predominated). And the philanthropic activities of local churches, which had given them so high a profile in the local community, became the responsibility of a declining middle-class group. Further, secular authorities offered increasingly professional alternatives in social work and education.

Confronted with these demographic and political changes, of which they were only seldom aware themselves, local churches soon became dispirited and saw themselves as 'failures'. The Victorian clergy of all denominations in Lambeth were convinced of the social importance of the churches: without them the moral base of society, and eventually society itself, would collapse. Confronted with change in the twentieth century they lost this confidence and experienced a crisis in morale: 'They no longer said that society would collapse without the churches. Instead, they constantly berated their bewildered congregations for their remoteness from the struggle for social reform, for their remoteness from the English people.'[24] Unwittingly they contributed to their own decline and confirmed judgments about secularization.

In the States I discovered a rather poignant example of churches being largely oblivious to demographic factors underlying their decline. Visiting Shaker villages in New England I was constantly informed that the demise of the Shakers was the result of religious changes in the modern world, a view shared by Shakers themselves. An increasingly secular society is keen to become tourists to Shaker villages and buyers of Shaker artefacts, but not to become members of this celibate utopian sect. As a result only a handful of elderly Shakers survive, with very occasional younger followers, whilst Shaker villages themselves thrive, albeit as museums. Secularization and modernity have apparently taken their toll.

Priscilla Brewer's careful examination of Census returns 1790–1900 (particularly suitable for self-contained communities) suggests a rather different explanation.[25] Founded in the 1780s, the movement grew in a general atmosphere of religious revivalism in New England until 1840. It then became increasingly female and polarized between young and old. It finally declined in absolute terms leaving a tiny remnant in the twentieth century.

Being a celibate movement it clearly could not pass on its beliefs to a future generation through the obvious means. At a time of revivalism from the 1780s to the 1830s it could grow through evangelism. Once this declined it relied instead upon adopting orphans and socializing them as Shakers. Its very success and popularity in doing this in the second half of the nineteenth century contributed to its own demise. A small, but declining, number of these orphans stayed within the movement on becoming adults. But even this form of recruitment was denied to the movement with a change of law at the turn of the twentieth century requiring orphans to be adopted within the religion of their natural parents. The predominantly female, socialized orphans that remained were ill-suited to return to the evangelistic methods of recruitment of their forebears. They had difficulty in maintaining even the day-to-day functions of their villages. So a polarized and declining movement now seemed destined to virtual extinction.

Not all of these factors are relevant to church decline everywhere in Britain. It is an axiom for the local historian that generalizations must be tested against the particularities of local data. In another outstanding local historical study of the social role and context of churches, James Obelkevich's *Religion and Rural Society: South Lindsey 1825–1875*, the author hints at other factors.[26] He too is sceptical in his study about secularization as an overall explanation. However he discovers a pattern in rural Lincolnshire somewhat different from that in Lambeth. Here it is not just the middle-class population that declines but the total population. And, although he sees a significant decline in the philanthropic function of the non-Conformist churches he does not find this in the Church of England. He also finds evidence of persisting unofficial forms of religion that owe little to institutional churches.

Obelkevich's data considerably increases the complexity of uncovering the factors leading to church decline. He is not finally convinced that South Lincolnshire was as fully Christian in the mid-nineteenth century as the comparative strength of the churches there might suggest. Certainly large amounts of money were spent during the period he studies on churches, vicarages and manses. Yet significant sections of the rural population owed as much to what he terms 'paganism' as to formal Christianity. Obelkevich concludes that the factors behind church decline are elusive.

II

My own research on rural churches in North Northumberland suggests that they may not all be quite so elusive as he suggests. Indeed, there are factors present in parts of his study which are insufficiently drawn together. He is aware of population decline and he is aware of increased spending upon church buildings in the crucial period he examines. By examining these two factors together and in rather closer detail he might have been able to offer a more cogent alternative to secularization. In my pilot study in North Northumberland I have discovered that the most vigorous period of church building over the last three hundred years was precisely that period when the total population started its ongoing decline. In terms of my projections rural churches which were half full in 1851 would only have been one quarter full in 1901. And this would have been the result of a combination of these two factors, not of any process of secularization.

My pilot study sought to examine the most measurable features of churches of all denominations in 14 Anglican parishes from the Restoration until the present day. The 14 adjacent parishes are in a naturally confined area with the Scottish Border and the Tweed to the North and the Cheviots to the West. They exclude any town areas, stopping well short of Alnwick to the south and Berwick upon Tweed to the east. The largest centre of population within them today is Wooler (2,034) and altogether their population in 1981 was 7,070. They are extremely rural, perhaps as rural as any set of parishes in England.

If four periods of time are compared (1661–1740; 1741–1820; 1821–1900; and 1901–1980) in terms of the physical presence of denominations, the third period emerges as a time of remarkable activity.

So, in the period 1661–1740 the Church of England was particularly active in a part of the country which had been so troubled by Border warfare (see Table 1). In 9 of the parishes an incumbent became resident and a new vicarage was built for him. One church was enlarged and 9 others were renovated. In addition 7 Dissenting (using the term technically simply to denote non-established denominations) chapels/churches were built, one was enlarged and 4 manses were built.

In the next period, 1741–1820 (see Table 2), 9 Church of England churches were renovated, 5 enlarged and one further parish first received a resident incumbent with a vicarage built especially for him. In addition, 4 Dissenting churches were built, 4 were enlarged, and 6 new manses were built.

However in the period, 1821–1900 (see Table 3), all but one of the 14 Church of England parishes renovated their parish church, all but 2 built new vicarages, 7 additional chapels or mission halls were built, and all the parishes now had their own resident incumbent (3 of which had populations of less than 300 and, in the case of one of these, of less than 200). Further, 15 new Dissenter churches were built, 3 were enlarged, 6 were renovated, and seven new manses were built.

In the final period, 1901–1980 (see Table 4), no new churches of any denomination were built or enlarged, although 7 Church of England churches were renovated, 3 vicarages were built and 3 Dissenting churches were renovated.

Yet the third period was characterized by a radical decline in the total population (see Table 5), a decline which has continued through the fourth period to the present. The high point of the population of this rural cluster of parishes was reached in 1851 (17,557): by 1901 it was 10,970; by 1951 it was 9,173; and by 1981 it was 7070. In short the churches expanded as the total population declined.

The physical results of this are only too obvious in the final period, 1901–1980 (see Table 6). Uniquely in this period in 8 Church of England parishes the incumbent ceased to be resident and the

Table 1 Church Expansion: 1661–1740

Parish	C of E incumbent first resident	C of E vicarage built	C of E parish church renovated	C of E parish church enlarged	C of E chapel/mission-hall built	Manse/Presbytery built	Dissenting church/chapel renovated	Dissenting church/chapel enlarged	Dissenting church/chapel built
Alnham			•						
Branxton									
Carham									•
Chatton	•	•	•						•
Chillingham	•	•	•						
Doddington									
Eglingham	•	•	•			•		•	•
Ford	•	•	•	•		•			•
Ilderton	•	•	•						
Ingram	•	•	•						
Kirknewton	•	•	•						
Lowick						•			•
Whittingham	•	•	•						•
Wooler	•	•				•			• •

Table 2 Church Expansion: 1741–1820

Parish	C of E incumbent first resident	C of E vicarage built	C of E parish church renovated	C of E parish church enlarged	C of E chapel/mission-hall built	Manse/Presbytery built	Dissenting church/chapel renovated	Dissenting church/chapel enlarged	Dissenting church/chapel built
Alnham			•						
Branxton									
Carham	•	•	•	•					
Chatton			•	•					
Chillingham			•						
Doddington									
Eglingham								•	•
Ford			•			•			
Ilderton			•	•					
Ingram			•						
Kirknewton									
Lowick			•	•		•		•	
Whittingham				•		•			•
Wooler		•	•			• • •		• •	• •

Table 3 Church Expansion: 1821–1900

Parish	C of E incumbent first resident	C of E vicarage built	C of E parish church renovated	C of E parish church enlarged	C of E chapel/mission-hall built	Manse/Presbytery built	Dissenting church/chapel renovated	Dissenting church/chapel enlarged	Dissenting church/chapel built
Alnham	●	●	●	●					
Branxton	●	●	●						●
Carham					●●				●
Chatton		●	●	●		●			●
Chillingham		●	●	●					
Doddington	●	●	●	●					●
Eglingham		●	●	●	●	●	●		
Ford		●	●	●	●●		●●		●●
Ilderton		●	●						
Ingram		●	●	●					
Kirknewton		●	●	●		●●			●●
Lowick	●	●	●			●	●	●	●●●●
Whittingham		●	●	●	●●	●	●		●
Wooler			●	●		●	●	●●	●●●

Table 4 Church Expansion: 1901–1980

Parish	C of E incumbent first resident	C of E vicarage built	C of E parish church renovated	C of E parish church enlarged	C of E chapel/mission-hall built	Manse/Presbytery built	Dissenting church/chapel renovated	Dissenting church/chapel enlarged	Dissenting church/chapel built
Alnham			●						
Branxton									
Carham									
Chatton									
Chillingham			●						
Doddington									
Eglingham			●						
Ford			●				●		
Ilderton									
Ingram			●						
Kirknewton									
Lowick							●		
Whittingham		●	●				●		
Wooler		● ●	●						

Table 5 — General Population Statistics

Parish	1801	1811	1821	1831	1841	1851	1861	1871	1881	1891	1901	1911	1921	1931	1941	1951	1961	1971	1981
Alnham	233	211	269	278	256	291	295	252	226	201	183	192	196	191	–	174	155	109	104
Branxton	209	261	253	249	261	284	255	234	221	222	165	175	184	171	–	196	162	138	133
Carham	1192	1316	1370	1174	1282	1362	1274	1210	1125	1043	906	910	841	779	–	638	560	414	329
Chatton	1135	1378	1460	1632	1725	1765	1651	1538	1302	1145	931	719	891	782	–	676	630	520	491
Chillingham	451	301	356	477	459	380	328	325	334	294	255	220	190	222	–	126	109	92	74
Doddington	734	887	865	903	941	825	795	762	642	726	630	695	676	590	–	509	464	373	323
Eglingham	1536	1538	1666	1805	1832	2000	1845	1631	1603	1562	1264	1279	1238	1194	–	1165	1078	898	873
Ford	1903	1860	1807	2110	2257	2322	2072	1841	1584	1435	1140	1051	950	977	–	781	775	662	529
Ilderton	475	502	574	602	604	641	598	528	476	471	434	390	395	361	–	311	261	236	227
Ingram	171	180	228	205	220	198	200	162	165	177	167	145	146	127	–	210	172	141	166
Kirknewton	1406	1472	1701	1674	1726	1732	1503	1402	1259	1234	1022	1050	1022	1055	–	996	810	736	648
Lowick	1382	1519	1799	1864	1941	1941	1946	1770	1513	1310	1138	1039	906	877	–	727	666	566	499
Whittingham	1465	1862	1749	1790	1896	1905	1923	1695	1575	1512	1399	1299	1299	1187	–	873	807	764	640
Wooler	1679	1704	1830	1926	1874	1911	1697	1610	1529	1301	1336	1382	1577	1505	–	1791	1976	1833	2034
Total Population	13,971	14,991	15,927	16,689	17,274	17,557	16,382	14,960	13,554	12,633	10,970	10,546	10,511	10,018	–	9173	8625	7482	7070

NB In the 1890s civil and ecclesiastical parishes begin to diverge slightly (also the latter sometimes change): for consistency these statistics adhere as closely as possible to the old ecclesiastical parishes.

Table 6   Church Decline: 1901–1980

Parish	C of E incumbent ceases to be resident	C of E vicarage sold	C of E chapel/ mission-hall closed	Manse/ Presbytery sold	Dissenting church/ chapel closed
Alnham	•	•			
Branxton	•	•			•
Carham	•	•	••		
Chatton	•	•		•	•
Chillingham	•	•			
Doddington	•	•			•
Eglingham					•
Ford			•	••	•••
Ilderton	•	•			
Ingram	•	•			
Kirknewton				••	•
Lowick				••	•
Whittingham			•	•	
Wooler				•••	••••

vicarage was sold, and 4 of their 7 chapels or mission halls were closed. Most dramatically, amongst the Dissenters 13 churches were closed and 11 manses were sold.

If the seating capacity of the churches is taken as an index to be measured against population an extraordinary and unexpected picture emerges. Basing the seating capacity of the churches on the incumbent/ministers' own returns to the 1851 Census (only one of which was an estimate by the returning officer) there were in 1851 11,034 seats in all the churches together to serve a total population of 17,557. In other words 63% of the total population could have been in church at any one time. This would certainly have pleased Horace Mann who compiled the report of the Census. He calculated that once you had allowed for the sick, the elderly, the very young, together with people to look after them, and, of course the servants (!), no more than 58% of the population could ever be expected to be in church at any one time.[27] Yet by 1901 this seating capacity had risen to 13,049 to serve a total population in the area of only 10,970 (see Tables 7 and 8). Of these seats the Dissenters had 8,704 and the Church of England 4,345 (a relative distribution well established elsewhere in England).[28]

There can be only one possible conclusion from this. Despite folk memories in the area, by the turn of the century churches simply could not have been full. An excess of church seating capacity over total population characterized the area from the 1890s right up until the 1970s. And the dramatic closures of the Dissenter churches (in this area predominantly Presbyterian) are obvious sequels of this excess.

This picture is confirmed even more strongly by examining the detailed returns of the congregations in the 1851 Census. At the morning services 31% of the total population was reported as being in church. In the afternoon or evening only 7.9% of the total population was in church. There is no way of telling whether these were the same people going to church twice or different people (it was a straightforward head-count). However if the morning congregations alone (which were presumably different people) are analysed it would seem from the returns that *in the ministers' own estimates* just under half of the available seats in churches were occupied. More specifically only 36.7% of Church of England seats were occupied at morning service, whereas 56.3% of Dissenting seats were similarly occupied.

Unless there was a dramatic rise in churchgoing between 1851 and 1901, churches which were half occupied in 1851 must have

Table 7 Population and Capacity of the Churches

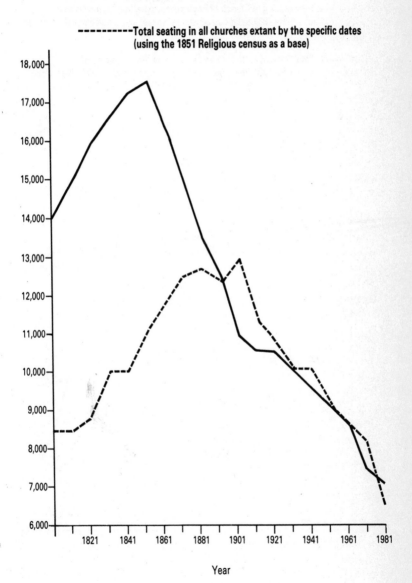

━━━━━Total population of the 14 parishes

----------Total seating in all churches extant by the specific dates
(using the 1851 Religious census as a base)

Table 8   Capacity of the Churches Compared

- - - - - - - - - **Total seating in Church of England churches by the specific dates (using the 1851 Religious census as a base) and predicting likely closures**

—————— **Total Seating in Dissenting churches by the specific dates (using the 1851 Religious census as a base) and predicting likely closures**

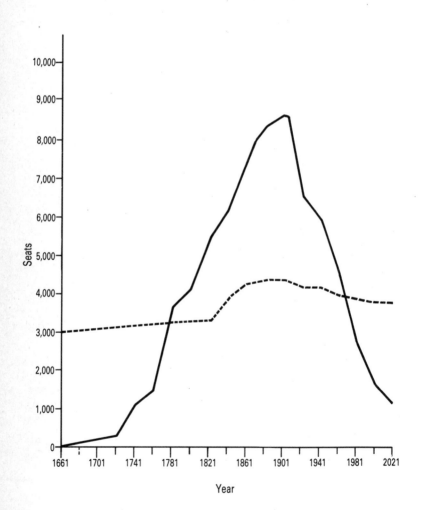

been considerably emptier in 1901. If the churchgoing rate had stayed steady, the dual effects of a decline in total population and an increased church capacity would have resulted in only 22.1% of the seats being occupied at the main service on a comparable Sunday in 1901. If the churchgoing rate had meantime declined the situation would clearly have been worse. I will examine the evidence about later churchgoing rates in the area in the next chapter. Even if there had have been a dramatic rise in churchgoing between these dates (a possibility which is not supported by the data I will produce), it would have to have reached Horace Mann's 58% of the total population for churches to have appeared as full, but no more, in the morning as they were in 1851. And in 1851, as I shall show in chapter 6, such a rate of churchgoing occurred only once in England.

At the end of his study Cox suggests:

> In England it was the actual collapse of the churches which allowed the complete triumph of the argument that religion is something which belongs to another age. The empty church is the single most important piece of evidence brought forth by people who argue that religion has become unimportant. They are right, but not for the reasons they think.[29]

Empty churches must have characterized this area for the whole of the twentieth century. In addition, church buildings being sold, vicarages and manses becoming private houses, parishes being amalgamated and clergy and ministers being lost to the area, all doubtless served to reinforce this argument. Yet all of this was predictable once the seating capacity of the churches exceeded the total population. The Dissenting churches particularly, without the protection of rural tithes, could not sustain such an excess. Their decline appears inevitable, without having to suppose any ineluctable process of secularization.

By 1901 there were no fewer than 45 churches in the 14 parishes serving the population of 10,970. Of these 21 belonged to the Church of England, 13 were Presbyterian, 4 were Methodist, 3 were Catholic, 2 were Baptist and 2 were Plymouth Brethren. But even this list does not reveal the full extent of the denominational competitiveness that encouraged the churches to provide an excess of seating capacity over population. In Wooler, with a population of 1336 in 1901 there were 3 large Presbyterian churches each representing a division within Scottish Presbyterianism. Together they could seat 2,080 people. The Church of England in Wooler, not to be outdone, enlarged the parish church to seat 800 and the Baptists and Catholics also provided small churches. It is hardly surprising that the largest of the Presbyterian churches, seating 1,030, which was lavishly rebuilt in 1868, was closed in 1903.

By 1988 there were 29 churches still functioning in the 14 parishes. Wooler now had only one Presbyterian church and there were just 3 other Presbyterian churches open elsewhere. The Methodists were reduced to 2 churches and the Catholics were selling one of their 3 churches, with the prospect of also selling a second. The Plymouth Brethren had replaced the Baptists in Wooler and had increased to three churches. The Baptists had disappeared altogether. By now real decline in church attendance was evident from a local Census conducted on Pentecost, 22 May 1988. The 31% of the total population in church at the main service in 1851 had been replaced by 8.3% in 1988 (excluding Sunday schools in both cases). Whereas Anglican attenders represented 8.3% of the population in 1851, by 1988 they were halved to 4.1%. However Dissenters had declined from 22.7% to 4.2%. And, despite the closure of 16 churches, the remaining churches were predominantly empty on a Sunday morning. The 49.3% of church seating that was filled at the main service in 1851 was only 8.9% filled in 1988 (Anglicans 7.6% and Dissenters 10.8%).

Behind these figures of decline lie a number of complex factors. The competition between a subsidized church and free-market denominations was clearly an unequal one. The latter rose dramatically and declined swiftly in response to the excess of church seating over population. Their demise and consequent loss of confidence was all the greater. In interview few local Presbyterians identified the demographic factors involved in their decline. Like academics they tended to blame secularization. Alternatively the problem was thought to lie with a lack of clergy – when in fact the total population per clergy had increased only from 605 to 707 over the years (see Table 9) – rather than with the more empirically demonstrable effects of clergy looking after three rather than one congregation.[30]

Naturally these factors cannot all be applied to church decline elsewhere, especially within an urban context. Newcastle City was growing until the 1920s and only started to decline in the 1950s, long after the decline of the churches there. But of course it is an axiom of this type of detailed socio-historical study that complex and differing explanations must be sought for the wide variety of situations that confront churches. I shall turn to this issue in detail in

Table 9 Comparison of 1851 Census with 1988 Local Census

(all church attendance comparisons relate to the main service in
1851 and 1988 : population census data for 1981 are used for 1988)

	1851	1988
Total attendances (– S. School)	5436	587
Attendances as % total population	31.0	8.3
Anglican attenders as % total population	8.2	4.1
Dissenter attenders as % total population	22.7	4.2
% attenders at Anglican services	26.6	49.7
% attenders at Dissenter services	73.4	50.3
Attendances as % church seating	49.3	8.9
Anglican attenders as % of Anglican church seating	36.7	7.6
Dissenter attenders as % of Dissenter church seating	56.3	10.8
Number of Sunday Schools	16	7
Number of Sunday School attendances	785	91
Number of Clergy (i.e. resident and stipendiary)	29	10
Total population per clergy	605	707
Total population per Anglican clergy	1097	1178
Total population per Dissenter clergy	1351	1768
Number of churches per clergy	1.03	2.90
Number of Anglican churches per Anglican clergy	0.88	2.83
Number of Dissenter churches per Dissenter clergy	1.23	3.00
Number of attendances per clergy	187.6	58.7
Number of Anglican church attendances per Anglican clergy	90.4	48.7
Number of Dissenter church attendances per Dissenter clergy	307.2	73.8

chapter 6. I believe that there is no shortcut, tempting as secularization theory has been in the past. Only by slowly building up a religious map of an entire region can we hope to understand church decline in all of its complexity. And it is indeed my hope to construct such a map for the North East, combining as it does remote rural and highly urbanized communities.

III

This is one half of my task. The other is more theological. I shall turn to this more fully in the next section. However, for the moment I am very conscious that my interest in church decline is not wholly dispassionate (is there really such a thing as wholly dispassionate research?). Corporate worship is at the centre of my ecclesiology and its demise during the twentieth century has always concerned me deeply.[31] Further my ambition is not simply to analyse church decline but to isolate means by which it might be countered. Of course these theological motives and aspirations will not be shared by all. It is perfectly possible to study church decline at an empirical level without them. I have learned much from social scientists and local historians who are personally indifferent to corporate worship. It is important to be as scientific, critical and tough-minded as possible if serious analysis is to be achieved. Nonetheless my own ultimate commitments are theological and I would be dishonest if I pretended otherwise.

In corporate worship I believe that we express and deepen our relationship to God. Theistic claims and language are, as I shall argue in chapter 8, by their nature elusive. They cannot be codified or captured any more than can the claims and terms of the artist, the musician, the poet or the lover. Although all can be depicted and analysed in cognitive terms those who engage seriously in them know that such terms are partial and ultimately inaccurate. There is no substitute for art, music, poetry or love, they can be known in depth only by those who immerse themselves within them. In my understanding of ecclesiology it is within corporate worship that we can really make sense of Christian signs and symbols.[32] Within corporate worship belief becomes commitment, words become the Word, actions become sacraments, singing becomes hymnody, and hopes become prayers.

On this theological understanding the gradual demise of corporate worship threatens the very lifeblood of Christian faith. Great music could, I suppose, survive without live or recorded concerts. Written music would survive and could be studied by those who had heard only musak. Poetry could be read oddly just as prose. Art could be viewed without feeling or passion as paint to protect a canvas. Religions too could be collected, studied and analysed without involvement or engagement. There are indeed those, particularly in the States, who believe (the term is not an accident) that this is the proper role of religious studies. My own understanding of applied Christian theology is quite opposite. Involvement and engagement are prerequisites and corporate worship is the pivot for this involvement and engagement.

Corporate worship is the centre but it is not the whole. Preceding it is outreach and following from it is social and moral action. For me an adequate ecclesiology is concerned about all three phases: the ways and means people are drawn into corporate worship; the quality and depth of that worship; and the challenges to social and moral action that arise from that worship. Aspects of each of these phases are measurable in empirical terms. Yet they are certainly not exhausted by them. At a more profound level each demands theological judgment. Not all ways and means of drawing people into corporate worship are acceptable theologically and not all social and moral actions, however legitimated by some forms of corporate worship, are theologically defensible. Theological wisdom requires a degree of critical distance as well as involvement and engagement.

Some might fear that an empirical project with such an overt theological motivation runs the risk of returning to the much despised religious sociology of the 1950s or to the even more vilified Christian sociology of the 1930s. For some years the sociology of religion has insisted upon retaining its purity by disdaining theologically motivated projects. It has done so only by distancing itself from other types of sociology. Few in medical sociology, industrial sociology, or even the sociology of race relations have thought that involvement or value-commitment is to be disdained. On the contrary they have cheerfully undertaken projects whose aim is to further successful medicine, industry or race relations. I believe that it is time for a more mature approach to the sociology of religion as well. Theological motivation is certainly not a requirement for sociology of religion, but neither need it be a disqualification. For me it would be unthinkable to study church decline without drawing in large measures from both sociology and theology. Applied Christian theology involves both perspectives, however uncomfortable this might be at times. It is good for theologians to be reminded of empirical realities and it might even be good for sociologists to be reminded of continuing theological commitments. Analysis and commitment need not be mutually incompatible. They can feed each other without devouring each other. However, for the next two chapters it is the empirical elements which must form my main focus.

5 · Competing Convictions and Declining Churches

The previous chapter suggested that rural church decline may be linked to excessive competition between churches in the context of a declining general population. Churches in North Northumberland increased their seating capacity in the second half of the nineteenth century – precisely at the time when the rural population was migrating to the cities.[1] Why did they do this? The only explanation offered so far has been in terms of inter-church competitiveness. The present chapter will seek to examine this explanation more deeply.

The evidence of inter-church competitiveness presented so far suggests that excessive rivalry between churches may in certain conditions contribute to their mutual decline. It has already been pointed out that this finding runs counter to the prevailing sociological orthodoxy[2] that it is active co-operation between churches which promotes decline. Divided and competing churches have usually been considered[3] to be stronger than ecumenically minded denominations. In this chapter I intend to test the claim that it was specifically ideological rivalry that contributed to the decline of the churches in North Northumberland.

Doubtless other factors also contributed to the extraordinary situation whereby churches continued to expand as the population declined. Victorian optimism and expansionism; emulation of the apparently necessary enlargement of urban churches in the late nineteenth century;[4] renewed interest in ecclesiastical architecture. Such intangible features may well have contributed. The otherwise very useful book *Churches and Churchgoers* suggests a range of possible variables.[5] Unfortunately it tests them in a very impressionistic manner and relies too heavily upon national membership figures rather than actual attendances. The advantage of ascribing the situation revealed in North Northumberland to ideological rivalry is that it is writ large, albeit unwittingly, throughout this crucial period in the submissions of the ministers of the various local churches.

I

In 1810 the Bishop of Durham apparently perceived three groups as presenting a threat to the Church of England, 'Papists', Dissenters and Sceptics. In *Queries Addressed to All Parochial Clergy within the Diocese of Durham at the Ordinary Visitation of the Lord Bishop of that Diocese*, the following questions were asked after ten initial questions about the structure, fabric and services of the Church of England churches:

11. Are there any reputed Papists in your Parish or Chapelry? How many, and of what Rank? Have any Persons been lately perverted to Popery; by whom; and by what means? Is there any place in your Parish, or Chapelry in which they assemble for Divine Worship, and where is it? Doth any Popish Priest reside in your Parish, or resort to it? And by what Name doth he go? Is there any Popish School or Seminary in your Parish?

12. Are there any Methodist, or Dissenting Meeting Houses in your Parish or Chapelry? What denomination of Methodists or Dissenters are most numerous in your Parish? What Methodist or Dissenting Preachers reside in your Parish? What are their Names? What is the Profession or Trade of each? Do they assemble in private Houses? And are they all licenced as the law directs? Is their Number greater, or less of late Years than formerly, according to your Observation; and by what Means? Are there any Persons in your Parish who profess to disregard Religion, or who commonly absent themselves from all public Worship of God?[6]

Clearly for the Bishop the 'Papists' were a central threat and the clergy were to be involved in the struggle to prevent individuals being 'perverted to Popery'. However, only three incumbents – at Wooler, Lowick and Whittingham – reported any significant numbers of 'Papists'. At Whittingham there were 128 with a Catholic chapel and priest at Callaly Hall (later castle). At Wooler there were about 20 with a resident Franciscan priest who met in a private chapel in the house of a Mrs Silvertop. At Lowick the incumbent, who lived at Kyloe and alternated morning and evening service between the two parishes, wrote:

We have never many communicants; for tho' the Dissenters frequently come to the Church, they never communicate with us. The Dissenters are more than ten to one in both Parishes: besides a number of papists. Our communicats seldom exceed thirty or forty . . . We have not above two or three Families of Fortune in either Parish. The better kind of Farmers are very punctual in their attendance on public worship, and our churches are very well attended. But I am sorry to say it, that the lower Orders of the People especially the Pitmen and Quarry Men, are very irregular in their conduct upon the Sabbath, and there is a great want of the restraining hand of an active Magistrate to correct the abuses of Lowick, particularly upon the Sundays.[7]

It is evident from this that Dissenters were thought to be a far more serious challenge to the Church of England in this area than Catholics. Every one of the incumbents reacted at some point to the strong presence of Presbyterians in the area or to the relative lack of a Church of England population. A few also believed that those who 'disregard religion' were a significant challenge. The incumbent at Ilderton spoke for others when he wrote:

There is not a Dissenting Meeting-House nor a Dissenting Preacher of any Denomination in this Parish; the only Dissenters in it are Presbyterians, who are so numerous as to amount to nine-tenths of the Inhabitants, tho' the number is not greater of late years than formerly. I do not know of any Persons who profess to Disregard Religion, but it is obvious that a Disregard to religion prevails every where in this Neighbourhood. More now than formerly, and many Persons too often absent themselves from all public Worship of God.[8]

The comparative weakness of the Established Church is also evident from the fact that most parishes, at best, had one service on a Sunday. Ilderton had a service only once a fortnight (the incumbent also served Alnham eight miles away up into the hills) and Branxton only once a month (the incumbent lived at Cornhill). The latter wrote to the Bishop that 'Children are catechised in Lent, but very few attend'.[9] Similarly the incumbent at Chatton wrote that 'There are so few children of the Church of England that no regular public Catechising has ever been established in the Parish'.[10] At Ford, Wooler, Lowick, Whittingham and Eglingham there were already Presbyterian churches. Reaction to the Presbyterians was ubiquitous: the vast majority of the working people were thought to be Presbyterians. Only the incumbent at Whittingham imagined that their presence was actually decreasing in the area.

By 1861 the Bishop of Durham's questions corresponded more closely to the ideological rivalry perceived by the clergy themselves. Questions about 'Papists' had been dropped altogether. Following the 1851 Religious Census there was now a new concern about the seating capacity of existing churches, the relative attendances of Church of England churches and Dissenting chapels, and the competing presence of Church of England and Dissenting schools and Sunday schools. The questions were distinctly more concise, as the following illustrates:

> 17. What is the number of persons
>   a: – who attend Church?
>   b: – who attend a dissenting Chapel?
>   c: – who neglect all public worship?
> 18. Is there a Dissenting Chapel in your parish and to what denomination does it belong?[11]

Most of the respondents gave statistical responses to question 17 (sadly based upon very varied criteria) and replied that few 'neglect all public worship'. The incumbent at Kirknewton responded at greater length:

> The Congregation varies considerably owing to the distances at which members of the Church of England live. At times also many Dissenters are present. The bulk of the population are Dissenters, chiefly Presbyterian, who attend very regularly their respective places of worship. Few but the sick and mothers with young families who neglect public worship.[12]

The vicar of Branxton, resident since 1839, now reported a congregation of 50–60 in the morning, with Presbyterians present in the evening taking attendance to 70–80 (1851 Census = 50 morning and 55 evening). Since his church only seated 93 it was clearly relatively full. Another small church Alnham (seating about 90) in a tiny parish reported an average year-round congregation of 56 (61 in 1861 Census) with a summer congregation of 70–80. The incumbent of Chillingham, with an attendance of 55 with 30 children (48 in morning and 15 in afternoon with 30–40 children in 1851 Census), reported that 'few, if any' neglect public worship altogether, 'tho' the attendance of many who tell me they go to the Meeting is, I fear, irregular and unfrequent'.[13]

By this date two further new questions appeared on the Clergy Visitation Returns:

32. As far as you are able to judge, has there been any improvement, or the contrary, in your Parish in the following particulars:
– Attendance on the means of Grace?
– Regard paid to obligation of Holy Matrimony?
– Drunkenness?
– Education?
– The physical condition of the labouring classes?
33. Is there any parochial matter which you wish to bring specially under my notice? or, can you detect any special hindrance to your ministerial success?[14]

Most of these issues were to feature prominently in subsequent Clergy Visitation Returns. The answers to them once more frequently highlight the differing social compositions of the Church of England churches and the Dissenting chapels and the strong ideological rivalry that clergy of the former felt about the latter. The incumbent of Chillingham again responded characteristically.

There has been a great improvement in the last few years. Attendance at Church has been trebled, and more than a proportionate increase in the number of Communicants, and Candidates for Confirmation, has taken place. With the exception of one man, we have very little, if any, drunkenness. Illegitimate children very rare. People have always been anxious for education and Lord Tankerville is building and improving cottages gradually.
  The special hindrance to ministerial success in all the Border Parishes is the lamentable extent of Presbyterian Dissent, the difficulty of dealing with which is much aggravated by the fluctuating nature of the population.[15]

The increase in churchgoing seemed marked since 1810 and greater than that which would have simply been due to the increase in general population (from 13,971 in 1801 to 17,557 in 1851, although by 1861 it had dropped to 16,382: see Table 5). Chillingham itself had actually declined from 451 people in 1801 to 328 in 1861. By 1866 all 14 incumbents held two services of a Sunday, with congregations of 20 or less at the second service reported only at Alnham, Carham, Ilderton and Kirknewton. All 14 parishes by now had their own resident incumbent. Yet each reacted at some point to what they clearly saw as the threat of Presbyterianism. As the latter flourished and as Presbyterian chapels continued to be built, reports of Presbyterians coming to Church of England services became rare.

In the 1866 Visitation Returns the clergy were asked 'Is there adequate provision in your Church for the poorer classes?'[16] Only the incumbent at Doddington, who reported a usual Sunday morning attendance of 200 for a church seating 210, and at Eglingham, reporting a morning attendance of 350 for a church seating 430, required more provision. The incumbent of Chillingham replied instead that 'There are so many Dissenters among the poor that there is at present adequate provision'.[17] All the others simply replied 'yes', the vicar of Wooler adding 'ample'. The latter was already experiencing acute.problems as a result of inter-church competitiveness. With Presbyterian seating in Wooler already amounting to 2,080 (according to the 1851 Census) for a population in 1861 of only 1,697 he evidently had problems. Not the least of his problems was that his own church had been renovated to seat 700–800 and he reported a usual Sunday morning attendance of 200–300 and 100 in the afternoon. Few of the incumbents thought that there had been any increase in church attendance in the previous five years. The incumbent of Ilderton was alone in stating 'There has been a considerable increase.'[18]

By 1870 all of the incumbents were convinced that there was indeed 'adequate provision in your church for the poorer classes'.[19] Even the incumbent of Doddington thought that it was 'sufficient as many of them are Presbyterian'.[20] The incumbent of Eglingham, having restored the previously ruinous Old Bewick chapel, was also convinced. No incumbent would now build or enlarge churches because of a felt lack of space for the congregation. Instead mission halls would soon be built to counter decline. A signal of this development is already present in the response of the vicar of Carham: 'All the sittings are appropriated, but owing to the fact that the church is a long way off the bulk of the parish and that most of the parishionners are Presbyterians, there is always room for the poorer classes.'[21]

In the 1874 Visitation Returns the question 'Is there adequate provision in the church for the poorer classes?'[22] is asked for the final time. All are thoroughly convinced that there is, and now the incumbent of Doddington adds, 'The unappropriated sittings are all accessible to the poor: and are seldom quite filled.'[23] The new question 'Does the attendance at church have a fair proportion of the population?'[24] reveals the full rivalry felt by the incumbents towards the Presbyterians. Ten of the incumbents specifically alluded to them in their replies. The incumbent at Chatton replied simply, 'No. From the large numbers of Presbyterians who attend chapel.' Similarly the rector of Ford responded, 'No. Three-fourths of the population being Nonconformist.' More pointedly the vicar of Lowick replied, 'No. The special hindrance is the great number of Presbyterians.' And the vicar of Wooler replied sadly, 'No as there are six Places of Worship *in addition to the Church*' (underlined).[25]

The Visitation Returns provide invaluable estimates of average church attendances during the 1860s, 1870s and 1880s.[26] If the figures for average attendance (where given) are taken from the 1851 Religious Census, in preference to the figures of actual attendance on Mothering Sunday, important comparisons can be made. Since the 1866 Return asked clergy to give separate estimated attendances for morning, afternoon and evening services, these provide the best comparitor. Table 10 indicates that there was a slight rise in rural churchgoing between 1851 and 1866. It also suggests that there was a subsequent drop in the 1870s and 1880s.

If those parishes are isolated which experienced both a sharp depopulation and additional church building, apparent decline can be seen. At the parish church in Ford in 1851 the rector estimated both the actual morning attendance on Mothering Sunday and the average morning attendance (excluding Sunday School) to be 300, in a building that was said to hold 410 people. By 1866, with an extra aisle added and with a chapel built to serve Etal, he still gave an estimate for the morning service of 300. However, he now added, 'perhaps this is overstated except on great occasions'.[27] By 1874 a new rector estimated morning attendance to be 175. At Wooler the vicar gave 200 as the morning attendance on Mothering Sunday and 300 as the average morning attendance in 1851. In 1866 the morning estimate was 200–300: by 1887 the estimate for total attendance of a Sunday was 200. At Eglingham 137 people were said to be present at the morning service in the parish church on Mothering Sunday and the estimate for average 1851 morning attendance was 250. This average estimate rose to 350 in 1866, but by 1887, with services held also in the restored chapel of Old Bewick and at Lilburn, morning attendance at the parish church was estimated at only 100.

Thus, despite the fact that Table 14 suggests that a slightly higher percentage of the population went to Church of England services in 1887 than in 1851, the three strongest churches in the area would have been visibly less well attended. A decline in the sheer numbers of

Table 10   Aggregated Average Attendances

Parish	1851	1866	1874	1878	1887
Alnham	62	80	67	67†	60
Branxton	115	140	120	80	70
Carham	75	44	30	35	130
Chatton	250	175	150	220	220
Chillingham	55	175	120	210	75
Doddington	116	350	150	150	90
Eglingham	320	440	400	445	260
Ford	370	390	305‡	240	240‡
Ilderton	45	45†	120	60	49
Ingram	28	90	40	35	40
Kirknewton	106	60	60†	120	200
Lowick	80*	240	120	120	100
Whittingham	270	305	305†	305†	305†
Wooler	450	350	250	350	200
Total index value	2342 13.3	2884 17.6	2237 15	2437 16.3	2039 15

* estimate by census enumerator.
† estimate based on previous return.
‡ includes estimate for Etal Church based on 1878 return.
Index value calculated by dividing total aggregated attendances by total population at beginning of decade.

Sources: 1851 Religious Census estimates of average attendance and similar estimates in Clergy Returns to Bishops of Durham, 1866–1878, and Newcastle, 1887, (excluding Sunday School attendance).

those attending (as distinct from the percentage of the population attending) is also indicated at Branxton, Chatton, and Doddington. Further, Sunday Schools may also have become thinner. The 1851 Religious Census gave an estimated Sunday School attendance at all of these churches of 540 (it may even have been slightly higher, since some churches, such as Alnham, combined Sunday School and adult attendance). The 1887 Visitational Return estimated the number to be 376.

Ideological rivalry was again evident in the 1891 Visitation Returns (by now for the Bishop of Newcastle). The question 'What are the chief hindrances to the success of your pastoral labours?'[28] produced many comments on the 'prevalence of Presbyterians' in the area. The vicar of Lowick again wrote pointedly, 'The struggle of Dissenters to keep their ministers: dislike to forms of prayer: jealousy of church: deep prejudice: neglect in the past.'[29] In a parish reduced in population from 1,946 in 1861 to 1,310 in 1891 and with four other churches in Lowick he was clearly feeling embattled. The rector of Ford gave the following three reasons:

1   That about ¾ of the population are Nonconformists.
2   That a large proportion of the parishionners migrate each
    year.
3   That Immorality abounds and the sense of sin is wanting.[30]

Several of the incumbents referred to the May migration (the 'May flitting') of agricultural workers prevalent in the area as a factor, but only one mentioned the general decline in the population. Most pointed to the Presbyterians. Five specifically mentioned 'indifference' as a factor. Indeed, there was now widespread recognition that church attendance was no longer increasing. In response to the question 'Has the attendance at church during the last three years increased?'[31] only the incumbents at Doddington, Eglingham and Ingram believed that it had.

The population of Carham had dropped from 1,362 in 1851 to 1,043 in 1891. The vicar was very conscious in 1891 of the 'hindrance' of 'Presbyterians – High criticism and low practice' and was evidently determined to change the situation. He reported that 'Divine service is held in a School room at the village of Wark, and in Mendrim (*sic*) School during summer. Cottage meetings in a kitchen at Old Learmouth and a cottage at Presson, and occasionally in a kitchen at New Moneylaws.'[32] By 1899 he established Mission chapels at Mindrum and Howburn and believed that attendance at worship was 'decidedly improved'. The bishop in his marginal comments was not so impressed, writing:

> Carham is a bad centre. Wark seems evidently given up to Presbyterianism. Mindrum gives encouragement and ought to have a resident clergyman, being 8 miles from Carham and 4 or 4½ from Kirknewton. W. Anderson has put up Mission Chapels at Howburn and Mindrum.[33]

William Anderson, the incumbent, died within months of the visitation and the bishop added that a new incumbent should do better there. Clearly inter-church rivalry persisted in the mind of the bishop who could still contemplate, even at this late date, a new parish in the area. Neither mentioned the radical decline in population. As noted in the previous chapter, these Mission chapels could only have taken further members of the congregation away from the parish church. Both were closed by the time the parish was subdivided to neighbouring parishes in 1954 (with a population of only 638 in 1951).

By 1899 the single question on church attendance was included only at the end of a series of questions on the moral behaviour of parishioners:

> 25. As far as you can judge, has the state of your parish improved or not in the last few years with regard to
> (a) Intemperance?
> (b) Sins of unchastity?
> (c) Gambling?
> (d) Observance of the Lord's Day?
> (e) Attendance at Divine Worship?[34]

Few of the incumbents thought that their parishioners were especially immoral, but equally only four of them (Alnham, Carham, Ilderton and Lowick) reported any improvement in attendance at church. The incumbent at Chatton saw a 'falling off markedly', that at Ingram reported 'the attendance at church is very thin', and the vicar of Whittingham suggested that 'country rides on a bicycle are too attractive to young men and the practice precludes attendance at church'. The rector of Ford commented, perhaps more accurately: 'There has been a general and very marked falling off in the attendances at Divine worship in this district but this applies to Nonconformists as well as to the church people and of course *the population is decreasing*' (underlined).[35] The bishop was again unimpressed and noted that 'The rector has lost touch with

the people . . . I am sure the people will respond to effort.'[36] He did
not mention the decline in the population of Ford from 2,322 in 1851
(the largest parish of the fourteen) to 1,435 in 1891 (and 1,140 in
1901).

The bishop himself evidently intended to continue inter-church
rivalry. After he visited Branxton he noted, 'This little parish is
admirably visited. A Methodist Chapel has affected Sunday Evening Services but there is no *automatic* dissent' (underlined).[37]
Branxton church had, of course, been reporting the presence of
Dissenters at its evening service since 1861, so it may not be too
surprising that the corrugated iron chapel, built in 1898 with a
membership of just fifteen, had not attracted all Dissenters. Again,
having visited Lowick he commented, 'Difficult parish to work
because so much dissent and so many chapels. The vicar works hard
against difficulties' and in a similar situation in Wooler he noted, 'A
good deal of nonconformity is in evidence'.[38]

By 1903 the vicar of Carham was distinctly more ambiguous
about the 'decidedly improved' rate of church attendance he had
noted four years before. The incumbent at Ilderton now commented tartly, 'I think it is encouraging if the attendance were as great
per cent in the towns the churches would have to be enlarged'.[39]
Only the vicar of Lowick remained convinced in both 1899 and 1903
that church attendances were still improving. Manifestly they were
not and most of the clergy reported in both Visitational Returns that
they were not.

This evidence clearly shows both a persisting inter-church rivalry
and an associated increase followed by a decrease in levels of
Church of England churchgoing. None of the clergy pointed out the
danger of combining high levels of church building in the face of a
declining population. Only a few even referred to the general
decline in population as a factor in the decline of their own and
neighbouring congregations. So fierce was the rivalry of the
incumbents towards the Presbyterians that the former tended to
blame the latter for many of their difficulties. Even by 1899 the
Bishop of Newcastle showed no clear understanding of the demographic features of the whole rural area which were by then well
established. His marginal notes demonstrate a strongly persisting
inter-church competitiveness. In the first half of the nineteenth
century this competitiveness may well have contributed to the
extraordinary growth of rural churchgoing. However by the end of
the century, in the context of a declining population, it can only
have led to its demise. Over-building must have contributed to

empty churches and empty churches contributed to the closing of churches and the closing of churches may have contributed (along with persisting empty churches) to a percentage decline in church-going. If perceived decline preceded actual decline, then competing convictions preceded perceived decline.

II

Local evidence from Presbyterian Church records suggests a very similar picture, with one crucial difference. If the Church of England clergy constantly referred to their Prebyterian neighbours, Presbyterian Kirk Session and Presbytery minutes scarcely ever mentioned the 'Episcopalians' (as they termed them). Their rivalries were predominantly internal and, perhaps for this reason, they were, like those engaged in civil wars, manifestly fiercer.

As with the Church of England there is evidence of early ideological opposition to Roman Catholicism. On 28 October 1839 the minutes of the Presbytery of Berwick recorded:

> The proposal to petition the Queen in regard to the appointment of Roman Catholics to official situations connected with the Government . . . after a long discussion of the whole matter Mr Watson moved that a humble and respectful petition be presented to the Queen, praying Her Majesty to consider the danger of calling Roman Catholics to her councils, and respectfully requesting her Majesty to reconsider especially the appointment of certain Roman Catholics recently to official situations in the cabinet and other responsible offices under the Government.[40]

In the event a more cautious counter-motion, suggesting that it was 'inexpedient' to make such a petition whilst the Roman Catholic Relief Bill was still in force, was carried. In contrast, petitions to the Queen were agreed by the Presbytery against the proposal to carry Royal Mail by train on the sabbath in 1841 and against persisting American slave ownership.

In 1843 another motion indicated inter-church rivalry, although again it was not finally adopted. It argued that in 'the intermarriage which from time to time takes place betwixt parties of our religious communion, and those of other denominations, the greater liberality of sentiment which prevails amongst us towards them than exists in them towards us is in such circumstances perverted to the diminution of our interests'. And it concluded that members involved should be 'influenced by views of religious principle than of convenience'.[41]

Given the jealousy of the Church of England clergy towards them, it may seem surprising that Presbyterian ministers left little evidence of reciprocation. In the context of a massive differential between their incomes and social status, it would not have been surprising. Whilst the rector of Ford in the 1870s enjoyed the enormous income of £1500, the minister of Crookham Presbyterian Church in the same parish was finding great difficulty in raising the recommended income of £205 from his church members. With an estimated morning attendance of 600 in 1851 and 200 in the evening, it was one of the strongest Presbyterian churches in North Northumberland. Even so its Kirk Session minutes[42] show a very considerable struggle to raise this money plus a viable income for the Presbyterian school teacher in Crookham.

Yet George M'Guffie's locally famous *The Priests of Etal*[43] provides no evidence of reciprocated jealousy. M'Guffie was Minister of the Etal Presbyterian Church (also in the Parish of Ford) from 1866 to 1892. In the introduction to the fourth edition of his book, M'Guffie referred at some length to the tribute to it written by Hastings Neville, rector of Ford 1872–1911, in the local book *Under a Border Tower*[44] that he in turn wrote. Specifically, M'Guffie cited Neville's comments that

> There is a book entitled *The Priests of Etal*, written by a former minister of the Presbyterians in that place; but do not suppose that this book contains an account of those who said masses for departed souls in the Chantry by the river-side . . . Nor must you expect to find in that work an account of the faithful labours of those who served as ministers of the present Chapel of St Mary, built and endowed by the devout Lady Augusta Fitz-Clarence . . . No, it is to the Presbyterian ministers that our friend's book refers, and in calling it *The Priests of Etal*, he only uses the usual language of the countryside, so that those for whom he intends it may understand its purport.[45]

Perhaps M'Guffie did not feel jealous of the Church of England because he had more of the attention of the local people than the Church of England. An analysis of the Communion Roll of the Lowick Scotch Church (as it termed itself) for 1858[46] shows that of those where the trade or profession of the householder is identified, 81 were professionals (mostly farmers), 23 were intermediate (stewards, etc), 126 were skilled manual workers (millers, cattle-dealers, joiners, etc) and 349, or 60.2%, were unskilled manual workers (described as 'labourers' or 'servants'). In terms of paid-up membership, at least, this really was a church of the people.

In contrast, the priest responsible for the St Mary's Chapel in Etal responded in 1874 to the bishop's question 'What is the average attendance?' with the stark response 'I do not count.' And in answer to the question 'Does the attendance at church have a fair proportion of the population?', he wrote 'Yes; to the *church* population; the bulk of the people are Presbyterian' (underlined).[47] The final chapter of *The Priests of Etal* even mentions *en passant* that, 'Lord and Lady Fitz-Clarence at one time were frequent worshippers' in the Presbyterian congregation. In the circumstances it may not be quite so surprising that rivalry was apparently felt more by the Church of England than by the Presbyterians.

However rivalry between Presbyterian churches and congregations was never far from the surface. Crookham Presbyterian Church was first built in 1745 as a result of a split within the congregation at Etal Presbyterian Church in 1732. For 35 years in the nineteenth century, although just three miles apart, they even belonged to different Presbyteries. Etal joined the Presbytery of Berwick in 1840, but Crookham did not join until 1875. And when declining membership and increasing costs forced the Crookham Deacons Court in 1868 to raise seat rents, they were clearly anxious that Etal should do so too:

> The Court unanimously resolved to express their Cordial Concurrence with the suggestions of the Presbytery, and to report to the Presbytery of Northumberland in terms of the same, stipulating that the 'Common Action', spoken of therein in the Rise and Equalization of seat Rents, in the bounds of Berwick and Northumberland Presbyteries, take place *simultaneously* within these bounds:– more especially in the congregation at Etal, immediately Contiguous to Crookham; And that this *simultaneous, common action* be arranged for from and after May day 1869.[48]

It is naturally a feature of free market denominations that they compete for members and watch their rivals carefully for signs of unfair competition. If the seat rents of one congregation were raised without a simultaneous raise in that of their nearest rivals, membership loss might occur. One disgruntled member of Crookham Church fought a considerable battle with the Kirk Session in 1873, demanding to pay his seat rent at the old rate since he believed that the new rate had been imposed illegally (he eventually paid). Others doubtless were simply lost to the congregation. One woman in 1865, who 'had given birth to an illegitimate child', refused to obey the conditions of discipline required by the Kirk Session (several cases came before it each year, and even more in the Lowick Scotch Church). After considerable discussion at several meetings of the Session, it was reported:

> The Kirk Session learned on the Report of the Minister and district Elder that Christina Hume had not once attended to the instructions of the Court on 18 June; and had, with the Council and Concurrence of her father and his family, received baptismal ordinances for her Child from the Episcopal Church. The Session, therefore, declared that their Church membership here ceased at 22 June last past.[49]

However such inter-church rivalry was quite overshadowed by the cloud effected by the Disruption within the Church of Scotland in 1843. The divisions of both Methodism in England and Presbyterianism in Scotland and Northumberland resulted in a very considerable heightening of inter-church rivalry and indeed of rival church building. It is this factor which seems to have largely caused the considerable extension of Presbyterian churches in the area in the second half of the nineteenth century. The normally bland minutes of the Presbytery of Berwick became considerably animated. In May 1844 William Grant, the minister of Tweedmouth, wrote a lengthy letter to the Presbytery explaining why he was leaving it. The style of this letter can be gathered from the following extract:

> The Synod, by most unnecessarily, and, as it appears to me, sinfully attacking the Church of Scotland, has done what tends to lessen the usefulness of their Ministers of that Church, by injuring their character; what may introduce the bitter and unholy dissension so long raging in Scotland, into England; and what may induce the Church of Scotland to adopt such measures as may cause the loss of a number of Chapels to the Synod and the Presbyterians of England. In many ways must the interests of the gospel and the Redeemer's Kingdom be thus injured.[50]

The Presbytery was evidently unprepared for this resignation and considerably bewildered by it, as the following extract from their even longer reply demonstrates:

> Does a mere difference of opinion in any case justify separation from those in church-fellowship with us? Have you not been more anxious in this case to separate from us than to do your duty?

Have you been at any pains to correct in us errors of opinion? Have you ever showed your credit by a show of effort? On the contrary, have you not with all possible haste, on the very first pretext offered for it, gone forth from your brethren without even an attempt to show to the world, that you were less able to act with them than heretofore; that your liberty was, in any degree, trammelled, or your conscience in the least point touched? Is not all aggravated by the consideration that the subject of difference belongs to a question on the several hearings of which you have all along professed to take the same views as those from whom you now separate, on the grounds of our opinion, supposed to be entertained by them of very minor importance, compared with the great leading views on the same question which you entertain in common with them? Now what will the world think of this conduct, so uncalled for, so useless, urged by no necessity, tending to no point – so self-willed, so wayward? What will the Church of the living God think of it? What would the Apostle Paul have thought of it, who decries divisions, and accounts it a heinous crime to break the unity of the Church?[51]

This was indeed animated writing for this Presbytery. Yet it did not persuade William Grant to return to its fold. A separate congregation and church was soon formed in Tweedmouth. In Lowick a rival congregation was formed in 1848 in an atmosphere of tension and even physical violence. And the Presbyterian churches in Wooler took differing sides in relation to the Scottish Disruption. Further, the United Presbyterians (who did not join the English Presbyterians until 1876) built a new church at Beaumont, within three miles of Crookham Presbyterian Church, in 1852. The English Presbyterians in turn built new churches at Horncliffe and Ancroft. In an area which already had sufficient Presbyterian churches for the needs of the population, even more were added, and they were added at the point when the population went into its present decline.

The effect of all of this is very evident from the Communion Roll and actual communions recorded at Crookham Church.[52] In 1851, the year before Beaumont Church was built, the Communion Roll recorded 825 names (with an estimated aggregated attendance of 800).[53] By 1856 this Roll was reduced to 740 (with an estimated attendance of 600).[54] In 1866 this was reduced to 419 (with 330 communions). In 1883 it had only 185 on the Roll and in 1889 this was reduced again to 165. The congregation, as already noted, by then showed signs of financial strain. In 1878 the Kirk Session recognized, as the rector of Ford later did replying to his bishop, that the financial problems resulted from 'the fact that this Congregation shares in the diminution arising in the general population of the locality. So that the Membership is not as great as when the Schedule of approximate Returns was rendered two years ago.' Neither they nor the rector of Ford apparently noticed that excessive church building, in the face of a declining population, had actually exacerbated this situation.

There were signs of widespread non-attendance of the remaining population in the area. In 1872 the Kirk Session at Crookham decided to arrange for 'the tolling of a bell at the church, to warn people off the street in front or adjacent to the church, with a view to the orderly assembly of the congregation and their decorous engagement *in all* the exercises of the sanctuary'. And in 1880 elders were instructed that, 'special attention be directed to the case of parents neglecting to bring their children with them to our own church worship, – more especially when within a walkable distance'.[55]

A new and popular minister helped to increase the Roll to 298 in 1900 (139 communions), although again it fell steadily to 234 in 1914 (107 communions) and to 184 in 1927 (average 77 communions). Perhaps surprisingly, in 1927 almost two-thirds of the communicants were men: of the total of 307 communions made at the quarterly services 194 (63.2%) were made by men. Of those who could have attended (i.e. who were not ill and did not die or leave the area in the year) 27.3% (17 men and 26 women) were absent from all of the services. Indeed, only 18.5% of those on the full 1927 Communion Roll (23 men and 11 women) made their communion at all four services. Further, 14.7% of those on the same Roll (11 men and 16 women) were absent for three years and 10.3% (9 men and 10 women) were recorded as absent for the next nine years. Clearly by this time a minority (predominantly men) were actively supporting the church. The church was completely rebuilt in 1934, considerably reducing its seating capacity, and this resulted in another upsurge of membership to 254 (average 120 communions). But by then the Etal Presbyterian Church had declined. The latter was to close altogether in 1948 with an octogenarian minister and little or no congregation. Of the 14 Etal members who transferred to Crookham in 1948 few attended the quarterly communion service at their new church (just 20 acts of communion over 12 services) and 6 did not even transfer for another two years.

By 1960 an apparently encouraging membership of 229 actually disguised the weakness of the Crookham congregation. Average communions at the four services in that year were 82 (36% of membership), the balance between the sexes had changed significantly (51.2% male), and Easter attendances between 1957 and 1962 averaged only 52. Average attendances on other Sundays were reportedly far lower – perhaps less than a twentieth of those reported in 1851. Yet even this was achieved only by extending the catchment area of the church further and further each decade. Even in 1948 there is evidence that it was already encroaching upon the area served by Beaumont (9 members were accepted on transfer from there in that year). In 1970, the membership of Crookham was down to 149, with an average of 73 communions (45.2% male).

The closure of Beaumont Church[56] in 1975 resulted in just 30 of its remaining 69 members (in 1961 it had 148 members) transferring to Crookham Church. However even these members were distinctly less active than they had been at Beaumont. In the eight final communion services at Beaumont in 1973 and 1974 these 30 members made 97 acts of communions: in the eight communion services at Crookham in 1975 and 1976 they made only 66 acts of communion.

The long-standing rivalry between Etal and Crookham and the membership problems associated with the building of Beaumont had ceased. Crookham now served the area once covered by all three churches. Yet by 1988 its attendance at Pentecost of 19 was just 2.1% of the combined Presbyterian attendances reported for the same area in 1851. The effects of church closures, a shared minister, and small, elderly and increasingly female congregations are only too obvious.

A very similar pattern is evident in those Presbyterian Churches that remained loyal to the Church of Scotland. Lowick Scotch Church[57] had 381 members on its Communion Roll at the end of 1848, the first year after the congregation split into two. The population of Lowick reached its height in 1861 (1946) before declining in 1871 (1770) and almost halving by 1921 (906). The Lowick Scotch Church reached its height in 1858 with 591 members: the Lowick English Presbyterian Church[58] reputedly had a membership also of nearly 500. By 1863 the Scotch Church was already declining with 563 members on the Roll and only two years later this had been reduced to 466. By 1877 the full effects of its rivalry with the other Presbyterian in Lowick were evident. Together the two churches had seating for 1,080 people (for a population by 1881 of just 1,513): but by now they had a rival Primitive Methodist Chapel, licensed in the previous year, a Roman Catholic Church built in

1861, and of course the Parish Church (and in the 1890s, with the population down to 1,310, they were all joined by a Plymouth Brethren Meeting House as well). The Annual Report of the Lowick Scotch Church for 1877–8 clearly shows the strain of all of this. It announced an ambitious refurnishing of the church at a cost of some £500, but admitted that the Communion Roll was down to 434 and that attendance and finances were poor.

> Throughout the past year the general attendance on the Sabbath at the regular service of the sanctuary has been unsatisfactory. From complaints heard from other congregations, the careless and sinful habit of neglecting public ordinances appears general throughout the district. Observation within our own communion too easily notes that many are very irregular and infrequent in their waiting upon the ordinances of God's House. Let it be remembered 'The Lord is with you while ye be with Him, and if ye seek Him He will be found of you; but if ye forsake Him, He will forsake you.'
>
> The financial statement at the close of the report shews that the sum of money at the disposal of the Trustees, is greatly insufficient to enable them to maintain ordinances as they have hitherto been doing. Bearing in mind that the roll of membership is still on the increase, and that there is no appreciable difference in the number of sittings let, the matter complained of must be due to either or both of the following causes, the irregularity of attendance already mentioned, and the diminution of the contributions given to the collections.[59]

The Report did not mention the falling population or, of course, the over-capacity of the existing church buildings. And the membership did not increase. By 1883 it was down to 255: the English Presbyterian Church in the 1880s[60] only had a membership of 180 and an income for all purposes of £120. By 1905 the Scotch Church membership was 235 (actual communions averaged 99), by 1912 it was 159 (average communions 64), and by 1920 it was 154 (average communions 38). This rate of decline was faster than that resulting solely from de-population: it represented actual church decline and not simply perceived decline. In 1858, at the high point of the Communion Roll, 30.3% of the total population of Lowick were members (naturally these population figures are approximate, since they are taken from the nearest Census, include children, and exclude populations outside the parish from which church members might have come) and over 50% of the same population belonged to one or other of the two Presbyterian churches. By 1863 this had declined to 28.9%, by 1865 to 24.0% and by 1883 to 16.9% (or some 29% for both churches). Similarly, average communion attendance in 1905 represented 8.7% of the total population, in 1912 it represented 6.2%, and in 1920 it represented just 4.2%. The attendance of 5 at Pentecost 1988, with the English Presbyterian Church long closed, was just 1% of the population and 0.8% of the combined Presbyterian attendance at Lowick reported in the 1851 Religious Census.

The refurnishing of the Lowick Scotch Church provided an unexpected offer from the rival English Presbyterian Church. The Kirk Session reported in May 1878 that a letter had been received from the latter's minister, 'in which he and his session liberally offered the use of their church to the Scotch Church congregation for worship during the interval in which the repairs on their church would go on. Gratification was expressed with this token of goodwill and Christian brotherhood and it was unanimously resolved to accept the kind offer and that the two congregations should worship together at the usual services.'[61] By now mutual decline had evidently dulled the bitter rivalries of the past. Nethertheless, the two congregations were not to merge for over fifty years. Even the 'unsatisfactory' finances of the Lowick Scotch Church did not persuade them to do this earlier. In 1878 total expenditure amounted to £227 (of which the minister's salary accounted for £188). Of this total amount £168 was raised through seat rents, a precarious resource in the context of a declining membership.

There can be little doubt that Presbyterianism, like the Church of England, in this area was in considerable decline by the turn of the century. A mark of the extent of this decline over the last hundred years can be seen in the relationship between average attendances and communions in the two churches. Returns to the bishop throughout the nineteenth and twentieth centuries sought information about attendance at communion. Taken by themselves they give a most misleading impression of general church attendance. So in 1810 and 1814[62] approximately 315 people in the area (2.1% of the population) were considered to be communicants and indeed received Easter communion: in 1857[63] there were estimated to be about 388 communicants (2.2% of the population): in 1887[64] the average number of communicants was estimated to be 238 (1.8% of the population): and in 1986[65] there were reported to be 667 Easter communions (9.4% of the population). However the crucial difference is that whereas communicants represented less than 17% of aggregated average attendances in the 1850s, in the 1980s in rural areas they represent more than double average attendances. So average attendances for the area in 1986 were given as just 251 (3.6% of the population). In urban areas the gap may be narrower: in Newcastle 1986 average attendances represented 2.1% of the population and Easter communions 3.1%. Amongst Presbyterians aggregated average attendances in the 1850s were also higher, although not so markedly, than communions. However, today, rural Presbyterians show the same pattern as Anglicans: communions represent at least twice average attendances. In both instances it may be the less committed church members (i.e. the non-communicants) who are now largely absent from public worship.

Another mark of decline is the collapse of the Sunday School. Branton Presbyterian Church[66] had a Sunday School of 215 children in ten classes in 1864 and a Bible Class of 46. In 1964, a decade before it closed, it had a single class with just 10 children. For all the churches in the 1851 Religious Census 785 Sunday School children were reported (the actual number, again, was probably higher, since many Presbyterian churches, including Branton, did not report their Sunday School attendances). In the 1988 Census there were just 91: with Sunday Schools run by only 7 of the 29 churches (see Table 9).

The closing of a large number of Presbyterian churches that has characterized the twentieth century was already predictable in the 1870s and possibly even in the 1860s. Yet Presbyterians continued to compete throughout this period. In all of my investigations I have only discovered one person who accurately diagnosed the situation. Significantly it was the minister of the first large church to close in the area, Tower Hill Presbyterian Church in Wooler. In his farewell sermon at the closure in 1903, the Revd J. McLeish analysed the situation as follows:

The church at Chatton was built in 1850, and drew away many members from the congregations in Wooler,[67] and in the following year the church at Beaumont Union[68] was built, and drew away members on the West side. During the last 50 or 40 years the rural population has greatly decreased, so that the congregations in Wooler have decreased in proportion. At one time, one of the congregations had more members than all the present three put together: Tower Hill, being the smallest of the three Presbyterian Churches, has been the least able to afford a diminution of its numbers, and the time has come when it was considered undesirable that it should continue a burden upon the funds of the Synod, as there was no probability that it would ever again reach a high degree of prosperity . . . Into the results of the ministry that is closing, I dare not enter. We have had our struggles, but never our strifes – we have had a stiff battle to fight for existence, we have fought it shoulder to shoulder and heart to heart. Peace and harmony have remained unbroken.[69]

III

By the 1870s the Primitive Methodists were also adding churches to the area and the Roman Catholics enlarged their churches at Lowick and Wooler and then Whittingham. An area already manifesting many signs of inter-church rivalry by the time of the 1851 Religious Census, was to become even more saturated with competing churches. The ideological rivalries underlying this are well in evidence from the records that they left.

They were certainly evident in the Catholic records of the 1840s and 1850s. The Pastoral Letter of the bishop responsible for the Northern District (including Durham and Northumberland) to his clergy in 1849 made this quite clear. The letter talked to the clergy of 'your increased zeal in the cause of religion' and of the needs 'of many poor missions, and for the establishment of others, which are much needed in various parts of our widely extended District'.[70] The returns of the 1851 Religious Census for Newcastle show that the priests of the two churches there felt themselves to be considerably extended with an estimated Catholic population of 10,000. Each church had two main masses and the congregations for these on average filled 82.9% of the seating. In contrast, seating in Church of England churches in Newcastle was only 66.2% occupied at a single service, with Presbyterians occupying 53.4%, Methodists 41.3%.

The term 'missions' to depict churches was no accident. The Pastoral Letter was not simply concerned with providing churches for an existing Catholic population following Catholic emanicipation. It was concerned with providing *the* means of salvation for all, as the following extract shows:

As Stewards of those possessions which a kind Providence has committed to your charge, you are bound to administer to the wants and necessities of your Brethren, and can you unconcernedly behold thousands of the Poor of Christ perishing for want of the Bread of Life, while you withhold those means which would effectually secure to them heavenly bread, and save them from eternal perdition?[71]

The Pastoral Letter mentioned no other denominations, but then since the Catholic Church alone possessed the Bread of Life this was surely unnecessary.

Given the pressing problems that the Catholic Church faced in urban areas such as Newcastle it may seem surprising that it expended so much energy building and servicing churches in North Northumberland. Local patronage seems to have been responsible in every case. The Lowick church (built in 1861) derived from the congregation of the Catholic family at Haggerston Castle. Whittingham (built 1881) derived from that at Callaly Castle. Wooler (built 1856) derived from the patronage and private chapel of Mrs Silvertop in Wooler. The surviving correspondence relating to Wooler indicates that there were considerable misgivings amongst the hierarchy about building a new church there. Thomas Gillon of Callaly, writing to Fr Hogarth of Darlington in March 1838, defended it as follows:

> The Property of St Ninians was left by the late Mrs Silvertop of Wooler to form a Mission for the benefit of the Catholics of that neighbourhood. She was frequently importuned both by the Bishop and Mr Eyre to leave the property to some other place, where it would be more beneficial, but to this she never would consent . . . saying that it was her decided resolution, that a Mission should be established at Wooler for the purpose of giving her family a chance of returning to the Church.[72]

She left a bequest of £2,400 to finance this. But by the 1850s it was inadequate. An appeal was launched in 1854, arguing more pragmatically that, 'A Chapel has, for some time, been needed in Wooler. The increase of Catholics, in this town, since the appointment of a resident Pastor, has rendered the present Chapel not only most inconvenient, but, from the heat and the impossibility of securing proper ventilation, almost insupportable in the summer months.'[73]

Unfortunately the Catholic population of Wooler was not as great as some imagined at the time. As already noted, back in 1810 the vicar of Wooler reported that it amounted to less than 20, meeting then in Mrs Silvertop's chapel. By December 1859 the priest at Wooler was writing to the bishop:

> The people here are so exceeding poor and – with the exception of Mr Henderson of Lowick and two poor families of the Watsons in Wooler – are truly wanderers . . . They reside here only whilst they can get work in the fields, and when that ceases – they set out and seek it elsewhere. Thus you will see that even were they able – they have not a permanent interest in the place.[74]

The 1850s had seen a determined attempt to evangelize in Wooler. In 1852[75] 20 'converts' were reported (and 4 at Callaly and none at Haggerston). In 1855, by which time there were 3 priests at Wooler, 56 'converts' were reported (one at Callaly and none at Haggerston). But in 1861 only 3 'converts' were reported (2 at Callaly and 8 at the new Lowick church). Wooler by then had already returned to having a single priest. Easter communions there rose from 23 in 1849, to 86 in 1852, and to 280 in 1855. But then they declined to 130 in 1861, to 72 in 1882 (with average attendance at Sunday Mass of 69), to 45 in 1892 (average 30), to 35 in 1899 (average 30). By 1907 it had climbed slightly to 70 (average 80). Even in 1859 the priest admitted to the bishop that the Catholic school in Wooler was struggling financially (just 30 of its 80 pupils could pay any fees) and by 1910 only Lowick church reported having a Sunday School (with 9 pupils).

Like all the other denominations the Catholics had over-built in the context of a declining population. The combined Easter communions for the 3 congregations amounted to 234 in 1849, reached a peak of 480 in 1855, but had declined to 297 in 1861, to 187 in 1892 and to just 109 in 1899, rising slightly to 177 in 1912. By the 1980s they had closed Lowick church altogether and seem on the point of closing Whittingham.

Exactly the same pattern of expansion followed by decline in the context of a diminishing population was evident amongst the Primitive Methodists. By the 1890s they had 5 churches in the area (Lowick, Milfield, Wooler, Ford Moss and Branxton). Today only Lowick and Milfield remain.

The Primitive Methodists[76] were the last of the four denominations to expand in the area. In 1867 they had a total membership of 126. This rose to 192 in 1870 and reached its highpoint of 260 in 1888. By 1900 it had reduced to 214 and by 1908 to 160. It served small mining communities in Lowick and Ford Moss and expanded and contracted with the industry. So at Ford Moss there were 44 members in 1870, but, with the introduction of better coal from the South by rail, it dropped to 22 in 1878 and to 12 in 1883. Lowick, in contrast rose from 31 in 1875 to 101 in 1878 (there was an influx of 39, virtually doubling the congregation, in March 1876), reaching its highpoint of 128 in 1888, and then declining steadily to 62 in 1908.

The congregation at Wooler well demonstrates the difficulty of trying to compete in an over-churched town. In 1867 they reported a membership of 45, but by 1878 this had declined to just 14. This increased to 55 in 1893, perhaps with the excitement of building a new church (it was completed in 1895). However by 1900 membership had declined to 47 and by 1908 to 35. Not surprisingly the Primitive Methodist Lowick Circuit Minutes show that the Wooler congregation was in debt in 1905. Today it has been sold as a hall to the United Reformed Church.

The little chapel at Branxton was one of the last to join the area. Built, as already mentioned, in 1898 with 15 members, it had already declined to 10 by the following year and to 3 by 1914. It was transferred to the Presbyterians in 1949–50 and ceased to function altogether by the 1970s. With its corrugated iron it visibly represented an over-stretched, precariously financed, and poorly attended church. It still stands (empty of course) as a symbol of churches irrationally competing in the face of a rapidly diminishing population.

IV

Burdened with the debris of nineteenth-century inter-church competitiveness it is hardly surprising that all of the churches in the area have declined in real terms. The very considerable surplus of church buildings ineluctably lead to three phenomena which are known to contribute to decline – closing churches, grouping several congregations under a single minister, and persisting with buildings that are too large for diminishing and largely elderly congregations. The twentieth century in this area is characterized by all three phenomena. And, as shown in the previous chapter, it is also characterized by a four-fold decline in churchgoing.

What is seldom realized is that all of these factors are interrelated. Once the competing convictions of the nineteenth century had resulted in far too many church buildings, those denominations which were working without a considerable rural financial subsidy (i.e. the non-Anglican churches) were forced to close churches and/or group together congregations under fewer and fewer ministers. Even the Catholics in the area have now done this. The Presbyterians have been doing it since the beginning of the century (notably with the closing of the massive Tower Hill Church in 1903). The small Baptist congregations at Ford and Wooler disappeared before 1900 and the Methodists are today struggling to survive at all.

The Church of England alone retains a sizeable presence in the area, and has increased its relative strength as a result from 26.6% of church attendances at the main service in 1851 to 49.7% in 1988 (see Table 9). Yet it does so only by grouping together more and more churches under a single priest or group of priests and then by heavily subsidizing them all. It even seems likely that this subsidy is increasing. After the removal of tithes before the Second World War and after the rapid inflation of the early 1970s no rural parish in the area is now self-supporting financially. Few raise even a quarter of the £18000 p.a. to diocesan quota that the Church Commissioners estimate is the true cost of maintaining an incumbent.

Independent empirical research would suggest that both closing churches[77] and grouping together churches under a single minister[78] are associated with a loss of church membership. Congregations do not readily transfer to other churches if their church is closed. And congregations decline once their minister is simultaneously responsible for three or more congregations. If in 1851 there was basically one congregation per minister, today there are three congregations per minister (see Table 9). And, as has been seen, the number of churches has been reduced from 45 in 1901 to 29 in 1988. These factors alone would be sufficient to effect real, rather than simply perceived, decline in overall churchgoing.

Because churches in the late twentieth century are simply trying to cope – closing churches when they have little alternative and grouping congregations together whenever possible – their existing congregations may themselves become an effective deterrent against general churchgoing. Most of the churches represented in Table 9 were visibly empty even at their main service at Pentecost 1988. For the spasmodic churchgoer it may be extremely difficult even to contemplate attending such churches. In 1851 spasmodic church-goers would have for the most part been able to merge into a large congregation (provided that they paid their seat rent or went to churches with free sittings). Today there are few large congregations. Elderly, sparse congregations were already reported from a number of churches by 1900. They possibly characterized most of the churches for the whole of the twentieth century. It is not difficult to see how they could have effected further decline in the general level of churchgoing in the area.

The evidence analysed in this and the previous chapter has deliberately focussed upon a small area in North Northumberland. Local study is, I have argued, the most accurate means of understanding the subtle dynamics of institutional churches. Yet to be of any real value insights gleaned from such study should be capable of wider application. In the next chapter I will tentatively suggest that there is evidence that inter-church competitiveness is an explanatory factor in analysing church decline elsewhere.

6 · The Effects of Competing Convictions

It is possible that the evidence offered in the last two chapters is unique to North Northumberland and does not in fact offer a reliable guide to church decline elsewhere. After all, the area was unusually troubled (for many centuries) by its proximity to the Scottish Border. English–Scottish wars in earlier times were replaced by Anglican/Presbyterian rivalries and also by inter-Presbyterian rivalries. Lowick and Wooler, with their plethora of Presbyterian and hard-pressed Anglican churches, symbolize this rivalry and suggest in the process that this might simply be a rather unusual area. Elsewhere in Britain rural churches might not have expanded whilst their populations declined, with all the inevitable problems facing twentieth-century churches that this has brought about.

More sensibly, churches elsewhere might have expanded only to meet the needs of burgeoning urban populations. The peculiarities of North Northumberland might have been the exception rather than the rule. In any case, as mentioned earlier, church decline in an urban context cannot readily be explained in the same way. Rapidly expanding urban populations apparently needed more churches, as the author of the Report of the 1851 Religious Census, Horace Mann,[1] insisted again and again, and inter-church competitiveness may well have helped churches to provide them. In short, the explanation offered so far may be extremely limited in its application.

If my thesis is to be adequately established it will be necessary to show that inter-church rivalry, vigorous church building, and a consequent excess of seating capacity over total population, characterized a wide variety of rural areas in the late nineteenth century as urban industrialization drew a once rural population into the cities. It is not of course a matter of dispute that in 1851 the population of Britain had only just ceased being predominantly rural and that today it is overwhelmingly urban. What is in dispute is whether churches widely competed to the point of over-capacity in the context of this diminishing rural population. In this chapter I will suggest that a careful analysis of the 1851 Religious Census does provide evidence that this was the case and that it even provides clues about how a modified version of the thesis might also be applied within an urban context.

I

James Obelkevich's *Religion and Rural Society: South Lindsey 1825–1875*[2] provides a convenient starting point. It has already been noted that some of the initial clues for my own research in North Northumberland were drawn from it. In contrast to studies of nineteenth century urban churches, it examines churches in a declining rural population. It also provides evidence for the substantial amounts of money that churches were spending on building during this period. And finally it points to the very considerable rivalry between the Church of England and the Methodists in rural Lincolnshire.

Obelkevich concludes his study with a consideration of whether or not it indicates a process of secularization in the area. Following David Martin[3] and Larry Shiner[4] he argues that 'the very notion of secularization is problematical, as it draws upon three separate sources of confusion: inconsistencies in the definition of religion itself, *a priori* theories of the drift of modern culture, and the practical difficulties inherent in the measurement and analysis of cultural change'.[5] These difficulties incline him against any 'inevitable' theory of secularization. Nevertheless, he does believe that certain cultural features of secularization were evident in the area:

> In the realm of formal religion a broad shift from religious to secular values was apparent in Methodism. In Primitive Methodism, for example, evangelism yielded to entertainment, the community of 'saints' to 'fellowship', and soul-making to character-building. There was nothing comparable in the Church of England, where the clergy's social gospel of paternalism and obedience was no novelty. The harvest thanksgiving represented a shift within the religious sphere from Christian to pagan rather than an instance of secularization. The decline of religious concerns appears to have gone further in Methodism – from a higher starting-point – than anywhere else in the religious scene, and is best documented.[6]

At the level of formal religious practice he also notes differences and rivalries between Anglicans and Methodists. In both denominations, 'the Religious Census showed that the overall levels of church attendance in South Lindsey were high'.[7] However, he believes that these high rates masked an underlying problem and tension:

Indeed a majority of the village population as a whole refused to make a serious commitment to either church or chapel. The clergy were pleased if the communicants in a parish amounted to 10% of the population: the same figure was the Methodists' target for membership. Even if both denominations had achieved their quotas in a given village, the great majority of the population would have remained outside, and as long as Methodists were in the habit of receiving communion in the parish church, the total elite group would have been even smaller. Probably the majority of attenders were the floaters seeking 'variety and novelty' rather than the salvation of their souls. Compared with the earlier period, the years after 1825 probably saw a rise in the level of church attendance, reflecting both the 'aggression' of the Methodists and the Anglican counter-attack . . . And in church and chapel alike congregations were subjected to unprecedented financial demands. Over-all demands, spiritual as well as financial, rose early in the century in Methodism, after 1850 in the Church of England, and perhaps declined after 1870, particularly in Methodism. But for most of the century the trend was clearly the opposite of secularizing.[8]

Obelkevich finally finds these differing features confusing in the context of a theory of secularization. The area he studies in the nineteenth century seems to exhibit competing tendencies of piety and 'superstition' and he offers no overall explanation of why the churches there eventually declined. Had he examined the 1851 Religious Census more carefully he might have done so.

If the three most rural registration districts of South Lindsey are analysed statistically from the Census, relative to a changing population, a much clearer picture emerges. In 1851 the adjacent districts of Horncastle, Spilsby and Louth had a combined population of 87,453. The area contained only two modest towns: that of Horncastle with a population of 4,921 and Louth with 10,467. Yet its land-mass accounted for almost a quarter of Lincolnshire (23.9%) and its population just over a fifth (21.5%). Today this remains a highly rural area, situated in the middle of the county but with the sea on its east coast. The population of this area had grown rapidly from 1801 (45,840), through 1821 (62,326) and reached its peak in 1861 (88,228). Even by 1861 two of the districts, Horncastle and Spilsby, had begun to decline: by 1871 Louth had also declined and the overall population of the three districts began its downward trend from 83,296 then to 72,569 in 1901. By 1971 it was 70,304 (54,462 without the towns of Horncastle and Louth) and represented just 14.9% of the county population.

The 1851 Religious Census shows that there was already a seating capacity in all of the churches in the three districts for 78,652. This was sufficient for 89.9% of the total population then. The Church of England churches alone could have accommodated 43.1% of the total population (37,702): this was considerably higher than the national average for the Church of England of 29.7%.

Bringing these two sets of information together, it is clear that the churches which were already in existence by 1851 could have accommodated 108.4% of the population in 1901. And this figure makes no allowance for the additional churches mentioned by Obelkevich built during the second half of the nineteenth century. The same churches by 1971 could have accommodated 111.9% of the population. Even in terms of the generous provision of church seating proposed by Horace Mann (58%),[9] by 1901 there may, with the additional churches, have been more than double this amount. The Church of England alone could have accommodated a notional 52.0%[10] of the 1901 population (and, in reality, far more, since the youngest members of this population would have been quite small!) and 53.6%[11] by 1971. Evidently the excess of seating capacity over population was as widespread in South Lindsey as it was in rural Northumberland.

Further, the 1851 Religious Census clearly shows that the existing churches were hardly full. In the Church of England total attendances filled: 28.4% of the seats available in the morning; 28.1% in the afternoon; and 7.2% in the evening. The Wesleyan Methodists were significantly better only in the evening: 24.4% in the morning; 27.0% in the afternoon; and 45.2% in the evening. After the Church of England they had the most seats available (24,047). The smaller Primitive Methodists (with 6,254 seats) were best able to fill them. But even they only achieved: 16.6% in the morning; 34.2% in the afternoon; and 58.0% in the evening. Thus, only in one denomination were churches even half-full at a single point in the day.

Again, supposing these three denominations built no more

churches in the area (despite the fact that we know that they did), and supposing that churchgoing did not decline in real terms (and again there are hints in Obelkevich that it did), churches in South Lindsey by 1901 would have been as empty as those in the projection for the same year for North Northumberland (see p. 75). Calculated proportionately for each denomination,[12] few services would have been a quarter-filled and none would have been half-filled at any point in the day. Church of England congregations would now only occupy: 23.5% of seats available in the morning; 23.3% of those in the afternoon; and 6.0% in the evening. Wesleyan Methodists congregations would now occupy: 20.2% in the morning; 22.4% in the afternoon; and 37.5% in the evening. And the Primitive Methodists congregations would occupy: 13.8% of seats available in the morning; 28.4% in the afternoon; and 48.2% in the evening.

These hypothetical, reduced attendances result solely from the excess of church seating capacity over a diminished population of this area. In reality the situation must have been far worse. These are deeply rural registration districts, yet they contain two small towns several times larger than any in the North Northumberland sample. This factor slightly masks the full extent of the rural depopulation in South Lindsey. And it makes no allowance for the extra churches that were added to the area 1851–1901. As a result, by the turn of the century churches in South Lindsey may have been even emptier than they were in North Northumberland. And it is not difficult to predict a twentieth-century pattern of churches being closed (especially those without the Anglican subsidy), ministers looking after several churches and congregations, and existing congregations becoming sparser and more elderly. In other words, all three of the factors that contribute to real, rather than just perceived, church decline.

Once this statistical analysis is added to Obelkevich's historical details – especially those confirming Anglican/Methodist and Wesleyan/Primitive rivalries and the building of extra churches after 1851 – it becomes evident without further detailed analysis that all of the ingredients were present in South Lindsey which have already been found in North Northumberland. It seems reasonable to supose, then, that inter-church rivalry led churches to provide too many seats for a diminishing population, and even to add to those seats after it should have been evident to them that the population was indeed diminishing. And none of this depends upon the supposedly unique features of the North Northumberland sample.

II

But did this happen elsewhere? The 1851 Religious Census again provides clear evidence that it did. Indeed, in 1851 there were 23 districts (out of 623) in England and Wales in which the seating capacity of the churches had already exceeded the population. In all but four of these districts this excess of seating over population would have remained in 1901 and, in most cases, become considerably worse.

Once the 1851 Religious Census is compared with the 1901 Population Census the extent of rural church over-capacity becomes evident. Table 11 shows the 84 districts in which the 1851 church seating would if boundaries remained comparable have exceeded the total population in 1901. Again, it should be stressed that this is a *minimum* chart: it is restricted to whole districts and takes no account of disparities between urban and rural church provision within districts. As a result, pockets of over-provision in countryside near large urban populations would escape this chart. Nevertheless it is quite sufficient to show that by 1901 there must have been a massive problem for existing churches within the countryside. Further, no less than 178 districts (28.6% of all districts)[13] would have had church seating in excess of 80% of their 1901 population. If late nineteenth-century church building in these districts resembled that in North Northumberland or South Lindsey, they might all have exceeded 100% by 1901.

The Glendale District in Northumberland (within which many of the parishes in my sample are situated) appears remarkable only because of its presence in the Northern Counties. The large industrial conurbations in Durham and Northumberland and the relatively low provision of churches in these two counties mask the extent of rural over-provision. For example, current research around Hexham[14] is showing that, outside mining areas, rural churches both expanded in the late nineteenth century and exceeded the total population by 1901. The average provision of church seating in 1851 in England and Wales was 57.0%. In Northumberland it was only 48.8% and in Durham 46.5%. In contrast, North Wales already had provision for 89.1%, North Riding for 87.0%, South Wales for 84.2%, and Cornwall for 78.7%.

Table 11 reveals several interesting clusters of adjacent districts in which 1851 church seating would have exceeded the population in 1901. In Suffolk, Hartismere, Hoxne and Bosmere had a combined population of 52,147 in 1851 which declined to 37,830 by 1901. The

Table 11 Registration Districts in which 1851 Church Seating would have Exceeded the Total Population in 1901

Registration District	1851 Seating as % 1851 total pop.	1851 Seating as % 1901 total pop.	Registration District	1851 Seating as % 1851 total pop.	1851 Seating as % 1901 total pop.
SOUTH EAST			NORTH MIDLANDS		
City of London	81.8	165.6	Lutterworth	75.5	110.8
Strand and St Martin	31.9	101.6	Billesdon	114.7	130.2
			Uppingham	84.0	104.2
SOUTH MIDLANDS			Horncastle	93.9	127.4
Buckingham	75.2	101.8	Louth	90.8	104.8
Brackley	85.3	109.5	Southwell	77.0	103.2
Brixworth	94.0	117.4	Bingham	89.6	105.8
Oundle	68.4	102.1			
St Ives	77.0	107.4	YORKSHIRE		
Caxton	84.4	111.2	Sedbergh	95.3	110.7
			Pocklington	95.5	112.1
EASTERN			Patrington	92.8	101.1
Cosford	89.6	109.2	Skirlaugh	113.1	112.1
Hartismere	76.2	107.3	Easingwold	90.1	104.0
Hoxne	64.6	100.6	Helmsley	101.2	126.5
Bosmere	86.2	105.3	Leyburn	101.9	151.8
Aylsham	93.2	109.4	Askrigg	125.9	157.5
Guiltcross	79.4	107.5	Reeth	92.8	256.6
Wayland	86.5	106.2			
Mitford	86.6	106.1	NORTH		
Walsingham	90.8	101.4	Glendale	69.2	113.2
Swaffham	78.7	102.3	Alston	71.9	156.6
			East Ward	100.3	103.7
SOUTH WEST					
Malmsbury	86.8	102.1	WALES		
Marlborough	99.1	120.3	Abergavenny	73.7	163.3
Bradford on Avon	85.5	103.6	Neath	63.7	110.8
Westbury	95.6	123.5	Llandovery	95.4	149.7
Warminster	83.3	120.7	Carmarthen	92.8	106.0
Tisbury	87.3	115.2	Narberth	88.3	112.6
Mere	71.7	116.1	Haverfordwest	86.1	102.3
Sturminster	85.7	100.9	Cardigan	104.4	139.0
Beaminster	83.7	130.0	Newcastle in Emlyn	98.7	109.7
Kingsbridge	89.8	119.0	Lampeter	104.9	111.9
South Molton	87.0	129.5	Aberayron	96.4	118.8
Torrington	82.4	115.3	Aberystwyth	100.5	111.2
Holsworthy	90.5	118.5	Builth	114.5	106.5
Stratton	97.7	114.5	Brecknock	105.5	122.6
Camelford	120.5	141.7	Crickhowell	92.4	100.5
Launceston	94.8	111.1	Hay	96.5	112.6
Bodmin	94.0	100.0	Knighton	81.6	184.7
Truro	83.9	105.5	Machynlleth	123.6	135.9
Scilly Isles	101.4	127.1	Montgomery	87.1	119.6
Langport	79.1	109.2	Llanfyllin	105.3	121.1
Wincanton	80.7	105.0	Ruthin	102.0	142.2
			Bala	109.1	128.2
WEST MIDLANDS			Dolgelly	116.0	100.5
Dursley	87.7	111.6	Pwllheli	110.6	110.0
Shipston on Stour	75.2	103.2	Anglesey	81.6	101.4

seating capacity of the churches in 1851 was 39,619: sufficient for
76.0% of the population. This was only slightly higher than the
Suffolk county average of 73.9%. Yet by 1901 this would have
accommodated 104.7% of the population of the three districts.
Some of the highest rates of churchgoing were found in Suffolk in
the 1851 Religious Census. Risbridge, with provision for 81.9% of
the population in its churches recorded a remarkable 58.1% of this
population at afternoon services, the highest for any district in
England or Wales, and Stow, with provision for 87.9%, recorded
53.6%, again in the afternoon. Naturally churches at these services
were fairly full: 70.9% at Risbridge and 61.0% at Stow. In 1851
attendance in the afternoon at Hartismere, Hoxne and Bosmere
was 40.6% of the population and the churches there were 53.3%
full. Yet by 1901 the same churchgoing rate in the same churches
would have meant that they were only 38.8% full. A rise of
afternoon churchgoing to 56% would have been needed to leave the
churches unaltered by 1901. Additional churches built in the three
districts after 1851 would of course have made the situation even
worse.

A very similar situation can be found in the adjacent Norfolk
districts of Loddon, Depwade, Guiltcross, Wayland, Mitford,
Walsingham, Docking and Freebridge Lynn. Their combined
population in 1851 was 149,352: by 1901 this had been reduced to
126,492. The 1851 churches could already accommodate 124,716,
space sufficient by 1901 for 98.6% of the population. In this context
the 107.5% accommodation for Guiltcross by 1901 is not particularly exceptional. In 1851 40.3% of the population of Guiltcross
were in church in the afternoon, occupying 50.7% of the available
seating. By 1901 the same churchgoing rate in those Guiltcross
churches would only have occupied 37.5% of the seating. To have
remained unchanged the afternoon churchgoing rate there would
have had to have risen to 55% of the 1901 population.

However, only a very considerable increase in churchgoing could
have left churches in North Riding unaltered between 1851 and
1901. The adjacent districts of Leyburn, Askrigg and Reeth are the
most remarkable in Table 11. Askrigg (later called Aysgarth) had
the highest provision of church seating of any district in the 1851
Religious Census and Reeth had the most remarkable population
decline. As a result, the three districts had a population of 22,512 in
1851 served by a total of 23,804 church seats, sufficient then for
105.7% of this population. They may well represent a stage further
on than North Northumberland since the population of the three

districts reached its height in 1831 (growing from 19,091 in 1801 to 23,313 in 1831). Thus it was already declining by the time of the Religious Census. Most remarkably Reeth reached its highest population in 1821 (7,480). By 1901 the population of all three districts amounted to only 13,773, with Reeth having just 2,520. If they were still served by the same 1851 churches, there would by 1901 have been space in them for 172.8% of the population. By 1971 their combined population was just 10,573, with space in the same churches for 225.1% of this population.

In 1851 afternoon was again the best attended time in the three districts, with 30.2% of the population in church, occupying 28.5% of available seating. By 1901 the same churchgoing rate in the same churches would have occupied just 17.5% of the seating. A sharp increase of afternoon churchgoing to 49% would have been needed to maintain the 1851 level of occupancy.

Interestingly, the provision of an over-abundance of churches in an area did not necessarily seem to increase levels of churchgoing even in 1851. Table 12 shows that Richmond, adjacent to Reeth, had seating for 78.5% of the population and very similar church-going rates as the other three districts. Since the Religious Census was a head-count it is necessary to assess churchgoing rates in three different ways. The minimum level of churchgoing in an area can be assessed by taking the busiest time of day in a district when church attendances across denominations are added together and then divided by the total population. Attendances then should represent separate people. The theoretical maximum level is provided by the index value,[15] which adds all attendances throughout the day and divides by the total population. Naturally this provides a much exaggerated figure in areas where multiple attendances were common (in Bedfordshire, total attendances actually exceeded total population). An intermediate means of comparing attendances is to take the busiest service separately for each denomination and then divide by the total population. Yet even this method may exaggerate attendances in country areas where it was common for dissenters to attend the Church of England (say) in the morning and their own church in the afternoon or evening. Whichever method is used Richmond appears little different from Leyburn, Askrigg or Reeth.

Braintree in Essex, with provision for 70.4% of the population, recorded a remarkable 53.3% of that population present in the afternoon. Halstead, also in Essex, had provision for 73.0% and a churchgoing rate of 49.3% in the afternoon. Only in parts of Wales

Table 12   North Riding with Stockton

Reg. District	% pop. at one church-time	% pop. at main service	Index value	% seats use: 1851	% seats use: 1901	seats as % of 1851 pop.	seats as % of 1901 pop.
Scarborough	27.8	34.8	67.3	40.8	84.6	85.4	41.1
Malton	19.7	28.9	56.2	33.1	29.3	87.2	98.6
Easingwold	28.1	38.5	70.2	42.7	37.0	90.1	104.0
Thirsk	32.7	37.7	72.3	40.3	40.2	93.5	93.9
Helmsley	24.0	28.2	63.9	27.9	22.3	101.2	126.5
Pickering	26.3	34.5	66.6	41.7	42.1	82.7	82.0
Whitby	31.2	36.7	71.6	38.5	38.7	95.4	94.7
Guisbrough	20.1	30.6	60.0	33.0	117.5	92.7	26.1
Stokesley	18.3	22.6	49.0	24.4	31.7	92.7	71.4
Northallerton	25.1	31.6	57.0	35.3	32.8	89.6	96.3
Bedale	30.6	42.1	79.1	48.0	45.1	87.7	93.4
Leyburn	26.9	30.4	66.1	29.9	20.0	101.9	151.8
Askrigg	31.4	37.0	67.1	29.4	23.5	125.9	157.5
Reeth	33.9	35.0	61.8	36.9	13.6	94.8	256.6
Richmond	30.7	35.0	66.3	44.7	37.8	78.3	92.5
Mean	27.1	33.6	65.0	36.4	41.1	93.3	105.8
Stockton	22.9	25.9	46.5	50.3	299.9	51.5	8.6

% pop. at one church-time refers to % of 1851 population attending church at the busiest time of day in each District: % pop. at main service is calculated separately for each denomination: index values are compiled by adding 1851 morning, afternoon and evening attendances and dividing by population: % seats use is calculated from attendance at main service in each denomination in 1851 and then related to 1901 population.

did an over-abundance of churches combine with high churchgoing rates. Aberystwyth in South Wales had provision in 1851 for 100.5% of the population and also had 51.8% of the population present in church in the evening. And most remarkably of all, Machynlleth had provision for 123.6% of its population in 1851, yet had 51.4% of this population in church in the evening with 41.1% of church seats occupied and it recorded the highest index value for Wales, 113.3. But to have sustained this occupancy in 1901 the evening churchgoing rate there would have had to have risen to 57%. Further, if the 1851 churches were still in existence in 1971, such has been the depopulation, they would have accommodated 351.2% of the population of Machynlleth.

There can be little doubt that rural England and Wales was already over-provided with churches by 1901. In those deeply rural areas which have continued to see depopulation throughout the twentieth century this over-provision has become considerably worse. Inevitably, it has resulted in the closing of churches, the grouping of churches under a single minister, and the slow demise of tiny congregations.

The full effects of rural depopulation can be seen in Table 12. The population of England and Wales experienced a remarkable expansion in the nineteenth century. In the first half it doubled and in the second it increased by 81%. In contrast, the first half of the twentieth century saw an increase of just 35% and the second half is likely to be very much lower than this. Dramatic as these nineteenth-century rises were, rural depopulation and urban expansion were far more so. The effects upon the churches can be seen from the last two columns in Table 12. There was already a considerable variety of church provision in North Riding by 1851. However, by 1901 the same churches would have been thoroughly inappropriate in at least half of the districts. If the whole is compared with Stockton – which adjoins Guisbrough and Stokesley and part of which (Middlesborough) became a district in North Riding – the contrast is clear. If Reeth would have been hopelessly over-provided with churches in 1901, Stockton would apparently have had far too few. In short, the massive shift of population from rural to urban areas caused problems for both rural and urban churches.

But was this over-provision of rural churches the product of inter-church competitiveness? Again the 1851 Religious Census provides evidence that it was. Westmorland offers a striking example. The adjacent districts of East Ward and West Ward had fairly similar churchgoing rates in the morning. East Ward, with a population of 13,660, had 25.5% of its population in church in the morning, 26.1% in the afternoon and 14.1% in the evening. West Ward, with a population of 8,155, had 23.0% of its population in church in the morning, although it had only 9.4% in the afternoon and 5.2% in the evening. Yet the most remarkable difference between the two districts is that East Ward had provision for 100.3% of its population in 1851 and West Ward provision for just 57.8%. The first of these districts had a total of 75 church buildings – 21 belonging to the Church of England, 4 to Independents (Congregationalists), 4 to Baptists, 1 to the Quakers, 18 to Wesleyan Methodists, 14 to Primitive Methodists, 12 to the Wesleyan Methodist Association and 1 undefined. West Ward, in contrast, had just 22 church buildings – 15 belonging to the Church of England, 2 to the Quakers, 4 to the Wesleyan Methodists and 1 to the Wesleyan Methodist Association. The result of this was that whereas 26% of the church seats were occupied in the first district at the main service, 39.9% were occupied in the second.

The 1851 Religious Census provides ample evidence that inter-church rivalry was present throughout England and Wales, in both urban and rural districts. There is not a single district where it is not present in some form. In Askrigg out of 33 church buildings only 6 belonged to the Church of England: the Independents had 9, the Wesleyan Methodists 8 and the Primitive Methodists 3. At neighbouring Reeth the Church of England had 5 to the Wesleyan Methodists 10 and the Independents 4. At Machynlleth the Anglicans had only 10 of the 66 church buildings: Calvinist Methodists had 20, Wesleyan Methodists 13, and Independents 16. At Guiltcross the Church of England had 20 of the church buildings, the Primitive Methodists 10, the Wesleyan Methodists 9, and the Baptists 5.

Indeed, in England and Wales in 1851 the Church of England had only 14,077 of the 34,467 church buildings. Rival English Methodists had 11,007, Independents 3,244 and Baptists 2,789. And the rate of church building was clearly accelerating. Between 1801 and 1811 1,224 churches were built: another 2,002 were added by 1821; 3,141 by 1831; 4,866 by 1841; and 5,594 by 1851. Sadly this expansion was not confined to urban areas. It also characterized the countryside providing it with church buildings well beyond the needs of its diminishing populations. The 1851 Religious Census provides a remarkable snap-shot of the mid-point in this process. Many rural areas clearly already had too many churches. Others, like North Northumberland, unwittingly had too many for the needs of its future population. Whatever other factors may have been involved, the decline of rural churchgoing in the twentieth century appears to be linked to the rivalries of the nineteenth century.

III

But what of the urban churches? There is a common assumption, even amongst sociologists,[16] that urban church decline does not need to be explained. Urbanization itself is regarded as a causal factor in church decline. On this assumption, if it can be shown, as I have tried to do so already, that the over-provision of rural churches in the context of a declining population resulted in factors (i.e. closing churches, amalgamating congregations, and persisting with diminishing congregations) which produced decline, then that is sufficient. The population largely shifted into cities and the latter are notoriously linked with poor church attendance. A once rural churchgoing population lost the habit in an urban context, as did the population remaining in the depopulating countryside.

Callum Brown has ably argued that the 1851 Religious Census provides abundant evidence that this assumption about urbanization is unjustified. On the basis of regression analysis of 1851 urban church attendances, he maintains that urban size is not a predictor of low churchgoing. Using the Religious Census for England and Wales, he has analysed the churchgoing statistics for 63 towns (aggregating morning, afternoon and evening attendances: unfortunately he does not quote results from any other method of assessing churchgoing rates) and has found that there is 'no statistically significant relationship between churchgoing rate and population size or growth for towns or cities'.[17] Only in the 53 Scottish towns (the data for which included smaller towns than that for England and Wales) has he found a significant relationship between the speed of growth, but not the actual size, of towns and low churchgoing rates. As a result he concludes:

> The Scottish result would seem to show that the problem for organized religion in the cities during the first half of the nineteenth century was *partly* the logistical failure in the construction of enough churches for the expanding population. As already noted, church-building caught up with or exceeded growth in urban population between 1850 and 1890 and, argu-

ably, increased the social significance of religion in British cities.[18]

Table 12 also provides a warning against the easy assumption that urbanization is a causal factor in church decline. The districts with the largest populations in 1851 – Stockton (52,934), Scarborough (24,615), Malton (23,128) and Whitby (21,592) – all had church-going rates higher than Stokesley (8,666). And Northumberland and Cumberland provided the two lowest churchgoing districts in England or Wales – both of them deeply rural areas – Haltwhistle and Longtown. Haltwhistle (7,286) in Northumberland had only 8.9% of its population in church at the busiest time of day, 11.9% at the main services (occupying 19.9% of the seats available) and its index value was 24.2. Even today Anglican churchgoing may be higher in urban Tynemouth than in the District of Haltwhistle. According to the 1986 Clergy Returns average attendance at Haltwhistle represented 2.3% of the total population, whereas in Tynemouth it represented 3.0%. Easter communions in the latter represented 4.7% of the population, whereas in Haltwhistle they represented 4.6%. In 1851 Longtown in Cumberland recorded the lowest index value anywhere of just 16.0%, with attendance rates at one time of 9.8% and at the main services of 11.1% (occupying 25.1% of the seats). With Brampton in between these two districts recording only marginally better levels of churchgoing (11.0% at one time: 12.4% at main services: and an index of 24.5) this part of the rural North represented quite remarkably low levels of church activity in 1851. The Municipal Boroughs of Carlisle (19.6% at one time: 20.3% at main services: and an index of 35.0) and Newcastle-upon-Tyne (21.3% at one time: 21.9% at main services: and an index of 40.0) had considerably higher rates of church attendance. Only Shoreditch in London (see Table 13) comes near to matching it. And, in contrast, the three highest churchgoing districts in London – the City, Wandsworth and Hampstead – recorded levels of churchgoing in excess of most of those for rural North Riding.

Much work remains to be done on present-day comparative rural/urban churchgoing rates, but it is possible that both the highest and the lowest rates are now to be found in urban areas. Whereas some urban priority areas report current levels of church-going of less than 1%,[19] a door-to-door parish questionnaire survey that I supervised of 818 residents in the affluent West End of Edinburgh in April 1974 produced surprisingly high results. 35.7%

of the sample claimed to go to church 'most weeks', 10.6% 'once-a-month', 7.7% 'festivals', 28.0% 'seldom', and only 12.3% 'never' (5.6% gave no answer). 6.0% of the sample were office-bearers in their church and 63.4% could name the specific church of which they claimed membership. Interestingly, two-thirds of the latter claimed membership of churches outside the parish surveyed. The extent to which affluent urban areas may still provide churchgoers for the rest of a city is at present little understood. It is possible that urban areas may in fact contain pockets of much higher churchgoing than a census of the most local churches in such areas would suggest. Conversely, churches in low churchgoing urban areas may be net importers of churchgoers,·in effect masking the real level of local churchgoing. In the Edinburgh sample only 7.8% specified that they had no religious affiliation. Even though the sample was skewed in favour of women (68.7%), and the registrar general's social classes I and II (35.0%), it was more balanced across age groups. In any event it would be hard to replicate such findings in rural areas.

Preliminary surveys undertaken in Northumberland provide similar evidence. A census carried out on the town of Morpeth in Northumberland on Mothering Sunday, 5 March 1989, showed a slightly higher churchgoing rate than that for North Northumberland on Pentecost 1988 (see Table 9). Morpeth has experienced continuous growth since 1801. It then had a population of 2,951 (total parish 3,574). By 1851 it was 4,102 (total parish 4,911). By 1901 it was 6,158 (total parish 8,609). By 1981 it had grown to 14,301 (or 17,584 including the now separate parishes of Hepscott and Ulgham). Whereas North Northumberland had a morning attendance (including Sunday school) in 1988 of 9.0%, an attendance at the main services of 9.3%, and an index of 10.7, Morpeth in 1989 had a morning attendance of 9.6% of its population, attendance at the main services of 9.7%, and an index of 11.0. Without doubt the main reason for this difference is the stronger presence of churchgoing Catholics in Morpeth. There they represent 45.0% of all church attendances: the Church of England 21.4%, the Methodists 15.3%, and the United Reformed Church 10.2%. The greatest decline since 1851 has been experienced by the last group: then Presbyterians and Independents (Congregationalists) represented 48.8% of all aggregated church attendances (Church of England 32.2%, Catholics 12.9%, and Methodists 6.0%). Morpeth has experienced real church decline since 1851 (when morning attendance represented 29.7% of its population, attendance at the main services 35.3%, with an index of 62.9), yet its churchgoing rates today, when compared with those for North Northumberland, do not support the theory that urbanization is a cause of this decline.

Again, North American patterns of churchgoing act as a warning against easy assumptions about the effects of urbanization upon churchgoing. It was noted earlier[20] that there was a considerable rise of churchgoing between 1880 and 1940, just as Britain was experiencing a quite opposite decline. Yet urbanization and rural depopulation have characterized both countries albeit at different periods of time. Whatever factors may account for this major difference – a subject of keen sociological debate – it cannot simply be urbanization.

If the evident decline of the churches in urban areas cannot be ascribed to the process of urbanization as such, what factors can be suggested? It is important to stress that sociological explanations of urban church decline are still in their infancy and must wait for more adequate data. Nevertheless, Table 13 suggests that some of the demographic features present in rural areas were also evident in Central London. Inner-city depopulation had already occurred there by 1901. The combined populations of Westminster and St James, Westminster, was 102,015 in 1851. By 1901 the now single district of Westminster had a population of just 33,087. St Giles reduced from 54,214 to 31,454 in the same period of time, Strand and St Martin-in-the-Fields (combined) from 69,100 to 21,669, and City of London from 55,932 to 27,639. The result, as can be seen, was an excess of church seating capacity over population in both Strand/St Martin and City of London, a near excess in Westminster/St James, and probably more seats than were actually required in St Giles.

Further, Central London had a long history of inter-church competitiveness (for which Pepys' Diaries provide seventeenth-century evidence). The City of London obviously had an abundance of Wren churches. By 1851 58 of its 78 active churches belonged to the Church of England. Yet it also had 14 other denominations competing with them (with traces of 65 Dissenter chapels active at some point in the eighteenth and early nineteenth centuries). Of the 74 churches active in 1851 in all the combined districts of Westminster/Strand, 44 belonged to the Church of England, 9 to the Independents, 2 to the Baptists, 2 to the Church of Scotland, 1 to the United Presbyterian Church, 4 to the Wesleyan Methodists, 1 to the Primitive Methodists, 2 to the Welsh Calvinistic Methodists, 3 to the Lutherans, 4 to the Roman Catholics, and 1 each to the Italian Reformers and Quakers.

Table 13 London – Selected Districts

Reg. District	% pop. at one church-time	% pop. at main service	Index value	% seats use: 1851	% seats use: 1901	seats as % of 1851 pop.	seats as % of 1901 pop.
Westminster and St James	21.9	22.2	42.2	69.4	22.5	31.5	97.2
St Giles	19.8	20.1	36.1	67.5	39.2	29.8	51.3
Strand and St Martin	19.6	19.9	35.0	61.4	19.3	31.9	101.6
City	36.4	37.3	62.6	45.6	22.5	81.8	165.6
Shoreditch	9.4	10.1	18.5	56.3	61.1	17.9	16.5
Southwark, St S.	15.9	16.7	35.9	68.5	395.4	24.4	5.8
Lambeth	17.3	17.4	32.2	69.6	150.9	25.0	11.5
Wandsworth	33.7	34.3	65.3	70.5	556.6	48.7	6.2
Croydon	27.9	28.0	54.9	69.6	423.9	40.2	6.6
Hampstead	39.5	41.8	69.2	86.3	589.7	48.4	7.1
Mean	24.1	24.8	45.2	66.5	228.1	38.0	46.9

categories and calculations as for Table 12.

Thus both of the factors that characterized rural England and Wales by 1901 – inter-church competitiveness and an excess of seating over population – also characterized Central London by the same date. Without any extra church building in these two areas between 1851 and 1901, churches already had a major problem by the turn of the century. This finding in itself may be crucial to understanding what might be termed the presumption of church decline that has been so strong a feature of opinion-makers, academics and the churches themselves throughout the twentieth century. Both Jeffrey Cox[21] and Callum Brown[22] argue that church leaders were amongst the first to make this presumption. Indeed, Cox, as was noted earlier, makes a connection between secular theories of secularization and the idealistic standards of Victorian evangelicals, for whom anything less than the total conversion of society represented 'failure'. However, given the fact that the Church of England, especially, was still a predominantly rural church by the end of the nineteenth century, a presumption of failure might be expected beyond the confines of the evangelicals. Churches evidently were in difficulties both in the rural areas and, it would seem, in the heart of the capital. Opinion-makers, too, in the form of Members of Parliament, might also have been impressed by the evident decline of the churches, since the two areas that they knew best were also rural Britain and Central London.

In such circumstances it is not difficult to see how the presumption of church decline might have arisen, perhaps even before urban churches generally really were declining. Certainly those social historians who have analysed local newspaper censuses of urban church attendance in 1881 and 1891 have tended to argue either[23] that churchgoing had remained steady since 1851 or[24] that it had actually increased. Nigel Yates is a slight exception in that he points out that, although the second half of the nineteenth century was characterized by energetic church building, potential congregations did not always materialize. Comparing 1851 and 1881 urban church attendance censuses he argues:

> In terms of numbers, of course, nearly everybody gained, simply because of the rapid rise in the population over the thirty years, though in Portsmouth there was a significant drop in the actual number of both baptist and independent or congregationalist attendances. In terms of the proportion of the population in church, though this is notoriously difficult to calculate, there may have been a more significant decline than has sometimes been

suggested, and this decline seems to have been universal, though it was more severe in some places than others. In Hull and Sheffield, as also at Bolton, Bristol and Coventry, it seems not to have been very great. At Portsmouth and Southampton the decline seems to have been more marked, though it was much greater still in Ipswich, Leicester, Northampton, Nottingham and Warrington.[25]

Whether these fluctuations would actually have been evident to the late Victorians themselves may at first seem more doubtful. Compared with the evident difficulties facing depopulating rural areas and Central London, urban churches elsewhere might have appeared still vibrant to most people, with large numbers of new churches being built to accommodate burgeoning populations. In any case Yates admits that churchgoing was not declining in all urban areas. Far more specific and detailed studies of urban areas will be necessary before a full analysis is possible here. Nevertheless, Table 13 suggests that population shifts were indeed creating problems both for inner London districts and for areas such as Wandsworth, Hampstead or Croydon. Areas which already had relatively high levels of churchgoing in 1851 experienced a massive increase of population by 1901. Wandsworth grew from 50,764 to 400,926; Hampstead from 11,986 to 81,942; and Croydon from 31,888 to 194,425. It was noted earlier that Cox believes that it was this growth of suburbia that may have deprived churches in Lambeth of their largely middle-class leadership and led to their demise in the first part of the twentieth century.[26]

The local census of 1881 for Newcastle[27] suggested that there was very little overall change in churchgoing from 1851. If in 1851, as just noted, attendances across denominations at the busiest time on a Sunday amounted to 21.3% of the population, in 1881 it was about 21.0%. Only the time changed significantly: in 1851 morning services were the best attended, whereas in 1881 evening services had become more popular. And if in 1851 the index value was 40.0, in 1881 it was similar. Yet there is other evidence which suggests a progressive weakness in the old central churches in the city. So, in 1851 the Church of England had 9 churches and 3 chapels serving the city: by 1887, as a result of a £100,000 diocesan appeal, it had 26 churches and a cluster of mission halls. Aggregated average adult attendances at these churches and halls was only slightly changed: 14.2% of the population in 1851 and 13.6% in 1887. Yet the congregations in all but one of the original churches were significantly thinner. The exception was St Nicholas which, in 1882, had become the cathedral for the new diocese. Most dramatically, aggregated average adult attendances had been reduced between 1851 and 1887 from 1,160 at All Saints to 250, from 800 at St Ann's to 270, and from 1,900 at St John's to 710.[28]

Despite all the as-yet-unknown features of urban church decline, there is already strong evidence that demography warrants more attention than it has received. The shift of population from being predominantly rural to being predominantly urban manifestly caused churches enormous problems in both areas. They responded by building churches vigorously in urban areas and only somewhat less vigorously in rural areas. It is usually assumed following Wickham's study of Sheffield[29] that urban church building was important to retain the church allegiance of the new urban populations. Even if most might regard the last nineteenth century rural church building as inappropriate, few would evaluate late nineteenth century urban church building in the same way. Again, this may be an assumption which requires testing.

It is commonly agreed that British Catholics have been the last major denomination to decline in Britain. They now probably represent over 40% of churchgoers in Scotland, and in England and Wales, despite being little more than 11%[30] of the total population, they seem to represent some 34% of churchgoers.[31] Indeed, the relative strength of Catholics amongst urban churchgoers today is one of the most distinctive differences from the churchgoing depicted in the 1851 Religious Census. In the latter, Catholics, who constituted then 5% of the total population, represented just 3.5% of all church attendances (morning, afternoon and evening aggregated), whereas Church of England attendances represented 47.4%.

To account for this major difference in churchgoing practice sociologists usually point to Irish immigration. Michael Hornsby-Smith's able study of English Catholics regards their largely immigrant status as a major factor shaping their distinctive behaviour and attitudes. As English Catholics lose this status so, he argues, will they lose much of their distinctiveness. For example, having given evidence pointing to growing disaffection amongst the young, he claims that 'the alienation of the working class has also become more apparent with the ending of large-scale immigration from Ireland; this had always given the Catholic Church the misleading appearance of being able to retain the allegiance of the working class'.[32] Without denying this factor altogether, it is not clear why it was this particular sort of (Catholic) immigration that should have resulted in such long-term differences of religious practice. Given that other sorts of (even Catholic) immigration from high churchgoing countries has not had a comparable effect, it is clearly not a sufficient explanation.

However, another distinctive feature that emerges from the 1851 Religious Census was that, whereas the Church of England had 14,077 churches (40.8% of all churches in existence then) with an average seating capacity of 377. Catholics had just 570 churches (1.7%) with an average seating capacity of 314. This feature has escaped almost unnoticed by sociologists. It is all the more remarkable when it is realized that some of these 570 churches were rural churches with comparatively thin congregations. In other words, urban Catholic churches expected to hold several masses on a Sunday and did not provide sufficient seating for all their churchgoers to attend at any one time. Unlike any other denomination in Britain this has remained Catholic practice throughout the twentieth century. In 1851 47.8% of Church of England seats were occupied on a Sunday morning, whereas 135.8% of Catholic seats were so occupied. In Morpeth today 4.7% of Anglican seats were occupied on Mothering Sunday (using 1851 estimates of seating capacity), whereas 277.5% of Catholic seats were so occupied. It is even possible that Episcopalians in parts of Scotland have more church seats than Catholics, despite having a tenth of their attendances. And in Newcastle average Catholic attendances may now be double those of Anglicans, yet the latter have four times as many churches.

It would, of course, be too crude to account for all differences of churchgoing practice on this basis. Yet urban church provision is surely a factor which requires further investigation. The Victorians made many assumptions about the relationship between church buildings and churchgoing. Today many remain heirs to these assumptions, in both rural and urban areas. Almost unnoticed, Catholics in urban Britain have worked on the basis of quite different assumptions.

IV

From this preliminary evidence it is possible to offer a series of predictions which can be tested, refined or discounted by further empirical research on church decline. Predictions are always risky, especially when so much empirical research remains to be done. Yet their heuristic value is precisely their ability to galvanize research: they are positions to test or to contest: they are essentially not dogmas to adopt uncritically. It is in this spirit that the following predictions of three broad stages of church decline are tentatively offered.

Contrary to most perceptions, the first stage of church decline may have occurred in highly rural areas and in Central London. From the 1870s or 1880s real church decline may have characterized both of these areas. Such 'real' decline should be detectable in two distinct ways. Individual congregations (especially those without an outside subsidy) may already by the 1870s be experiencing financial, membership and attendance difficulties. And secondly a declining proportion of the population may be actively involved in the churches. New church building will effectively stop in these areas by or before the turn of the century, followed soon after by extensive closure of churches. Each closure will tend to be heralded by a loss of church membership and will be followed by real decline, since members will largely fail to become effective members of other congregations. Typically, once a church starts to decline, its members become increasingly disaffected, and then, once it closes, these disaffected members either become non-attending members of another church or cease to be members of any church. A less dramatic pattern of churches with small congregations remaining open, but sharing a minister with other churches, will also be increasingly found in both of these areas. This too will be associated with decline, but perhaps not such rapid decline as that following church closures. Finally, after a century of decline rural churches today will be found to have churchgoing rates significantly lower than many middle-class urban or suburban areas: small congregations in large church buildings will characterize rural areas and indeed contribute to their own decline.

In the second stage urban churches more widely started to decline in relation to the population, often after the turn of the century, although some of the larger central churches (and especially the Church of England in London)[33] were already struggling by the 1880s. They declined first in those areas, such as Lambeth, which, despite a growing population, may have experienced a significant exmigration of middle-class leadership, or in those, such as Hampstead or Wandsworth, which experienced a very rapid growth of population. In contrast, pockets of middle-class urban and suburban areas may not have declined until the 1960s (if then). Urban decline for the most part may have resulted from a number of demographic factors: actual depopulation in city centres; middle-class exmigration to suburbia: unusually rapid urban growth;

immigration of people from inner-city and rural areas who had already lost effective contact with the churches. It will have been resisted most strongly by those urban denominations which provided a minimum of church accommodation (and thus fuller individual congregations).

In the third stage, once church decline was evident within rural areas and within some urban areas, cultural factors also became important. Some would depict these factors by the term 'secularization'. I have preferred instead the rather tighter term 'presumption of church decline', the prevalence of which can at least be tested through examining contemporary records. Once this presumption became widely established, it in turn encouraged disaffection from the churches. For example, Sunday Schools, so widespread in Victorian society, found problems in recruiting teachers and then problems in retaining children beyond puberty. This presumption has now also affected British Catholics – the last major denomination to decline – and may in addition have affected the remaining pockets of urban and suburban middle-class churchgoers. Culture rather than demography (albeit culture affected by prior changes in demography) may be a more important factor in explaining the comparatively recent church decline to be found amongst the latter.

Underlying this scenario is the contention that denominations competed to their mutual disadvantage largely disregarding demographic factors. Given the fact that Anglicans, Catholics, Methodists and the United Reformed Church (or Presbyterians in Scotland) still attempt to provide separate 'coverage' in scattered rural communities today, mutually disadvantageous competition may not have ceased. Indeed, all of these denominations subsidize (through one means or another) this continuing rural 'coverage', none more so than the Church of England. Further, extensive empirical research is needed to test whether the apparent growth of evangelical churches and house-groups in Britain today is the result of transferred church membership (and thus competing convictions) or new membership. Indeed, very little is known about the social and physical locations of these members. Yet such information is obviously vital for future strategy within churches.

There are signs, though, that mutual disadvantage may be encouraging less competitiveness amongst some churches today. Denominations sharing buildings can now be encountered both in rural areas and in new housing estates. Further, concern about urban priority areas is currently fostering inter-church social and welfare action. Given the weakness of all churches in urban priority areas, it is possible that new congregations started within them are less committed to existing, competing church structures. And, as academic theology becomes more seriously ecumenical in Britain, so ordinands may themselves be less inclined to perpetuate past rivalries. This, however, is the theme of the next chapter.

PART THREE

Theology and Competing Convictions

7 · Relativism in Modern Theology

Competing theological convictions seem to be resurgent within parts of the modern world as once they were in Victorian churches, yet ironically modern theology is being increasingly pulled in the opposite direction. In the latter it is relativism, rather than competing convictions, which is seen as a major challenge. Structural and cultural changes within modern theology face it at almost every point with relativism. In this chapter I will explore some of these changes before sketching in the next an understanding of how theology might take them fully into account.

The gulf between modern theology and present-day fundamentalism will already be apparent from chapters 2 and 3. They argued that fundamentalism, although currently resurgent, is also a counter-cultural phenomenon. It is not simply a movement, or series of movements, based upon scriptural absolutism. Fundamentalism is essentially modern in that it is a post-critical reaction. Those who identify themselves as fundamentalists, across a number of quite different religious traditions, also see themselves as combating key features of modernity. So 'creationism' amongst American Protestant fundamentalists is not simply a return to old-style biblical belief. It is self-consciously an alternative to Darwinianism and is intended to be taught as such. It is Darwinianism, not Genesis, which controls the debate, and it is scientific data (fossil evidence, species development, etc) whch is paramount rather than biblical exegesis.

In so far as fundamentalism is essentially counter-cultural, it is quite opposite to modern theology. It has always been a feature of systematic theology that it works broadly within the parameters of modern culture. At least since Augustine, it has tended to rely for its own understanding upon contemporary intellectual culture. At one point or another, neo-Platonism, Aristotelianism, idealism, existentialism (and indeed many other philosophical movements) have been deliberately adopted by theologians. Whatever the dominant philosophical ethos systematic theologians have frequently regarded it as important that they use each ethos to interpret theology itself, even when they are aware that this ethos will soon be replaced by another. They do this perhaps, partly because they wish to engage with contemporary intelligence, and partly because they simply are themselves a part of that intelligence.

Fundamentalists, in contrast, are characteristically dismissive of this whole theological enterprise and yearn for a less sophisticated purity of belief. This may be a part of their appeal. Belief appears all too complicated and implicated once left in the hands of the theologian. Countless variables are introduced and the very framework of conviction seems to be undermined in the process. The theologian who is sensitive to the quixotic nature of past convictions and to the changing contexts of present convictions, appears to be relativized by these very sensitivities. The fundamentalist, instead, seeks to return to a 'simple faith', to a faith unclouded by academic niceties and compromises.

Yet to the theologian the fundamentalist can achieve this only by ignoring evidence, even evidence of inconsistency within fundamentalism. It was noted earlier that fundamentalists within both Iran and North America have frequently denounced the evil of television in the modern world, even whilst systematically exploiting it themselves. They have demanded unswerving obedience to scriptural absolutism, even whilst reserving for themselves the right to interpret scripture. And they have derided secular intellectualism, even whilst employing their own forms of intellectualism. Far from being 'pure' and 'simple' versions of faith, they are permanently attempting to control the pluralism of absolutist convictions within their own ranks. It is not just the Mullahs in Iran who must coerce conviction in the context of potential ideological anarchy, the American tele-evangelists have patently been just as anxious to enforce hegemony.

Again, modern theology is deeply at odds with the competing convictions uncovered in the last three chapters. Churches mutually competing to the point of over-capacity is so counter-intuitive in modern terms, that it has been necessary to rehearse the evidence for it as fully as possible. Only by doing this does the full extent of past ecclesiastical antagonisms become evident. Presbyterians were regarded by Anglicans as grave 'hindrances'. Anglicans were simply ignored by Presbyterians who were themselves too preoccupied with bitter internal schisms. Catholics simply assumed that they alone possessed the 'bread of life' essential to eternal salvation. Echoes of all of these positions can still be found amongst these churches today. Yet they are echoes, not the full-blooded voices from which they sprang. Conversionist sects, rather than churches, are more likely to maintain such voices in modern Britain.

In parts of the developing world competing convictions between churches are still apparent. In some countries within South America or in South Korea, for example, where populations and churches are still growing, there is already evidence of deep antagonisms between and within churches. Liberation theology and apolitical evangelicalism often compete for the same ground, dividing churches and communities. It is not difficult to imagine that a few years hence, when population growth slows down and when certain areas depopulate, churches themselves will 'mysteriously' start to decline. At least one of the ingredients underlying decline – namely bitter inter-church rivalry – seems to be present. If it blinds churches to demographic shifts, then the pattern of Victorian church decline may be replicated once again. What so often appears today as a sign of vitality in world-wide Christianity may actually be the harbinger of further decline.

Sociology has so far played a dominant role in my analysis. There have been hints at times of underlying theological commitments, which will come to the fore in the next chapter, yet for the moment they have been *sote voce*. The *fortissimo* of sociological analysis may already be theologically disturbing. To argue that rural church decline resulted from competing convictions in a context of depopulation may be comforting to churchpeople at one level. After all it avoids the ideological inevitability of some ineluctable process of secularization. However it may be a source of comfort which is fairly short lived. Demographic explanations may appear even more deterministic than those assuming such a process of secularization. They run even more counter to the perceptions of the churches themselves and they suggest, in the end, that it is demographic factors rather than ostensive beliefs which have most shaped particular denominations.

Again, to argue that fundamentalism is essentially a counter-culture may initially be comforting to denominations which see themselves as more mainstream. Fundamentalist groups may be less impressed. Doubtless they would be singularly unimpressed with any amount of sociological observation of similarities between mutually hostile forms of fundamentalism. Indeed, as argued in chapter 2, to adopt a fully sociological approach to fundamentalism is already to undermine the absolutism which sustains it as a counter-culture. However such an approach may also finally disconcert more conventional denominations. Deep commitments seem to be reduced thereby to passing opinions: absolutism is replaced with ever receding relativism: and sincerely held religious convictions are treated as epiphenomenally as they are by secularization theorists.

In short, the problem of methodological relativism outlined in chapter 1 seems to be writ large in the last five chapters. Further it seems to be sociology which is the *bête noire*. Whilst it apparently offers an enhanced understanding of religious institutions, it seems at the same time to undermine and relativize them. In the circumstances it might be safer for theologians to return to the more traditional delights of philosophy and history!

Tempting as such an escape might be, it misses an obvious point. The increasing use of the social sciences by theologians is more a symptom than a cause of present-day theological pluralism and the sense of relativism that it tends to engender. For the most part theologians have not turned to the social sciences because they wish to undermine theological convictions. There have in the past been clear polemical uses of social perspectives of one sort or another. In the present, however, increasing theological uses of sociology have been characteristically inquisitive rather than polemical. They may result more from an observation of existing pluralism and a concern to account for it adequately, than from any desire to 'disturb the faithful'.

The Dominican theologian Edward Schillebeeckx provides a very obvious example of this. More traditional Catholics have sometimes accounted for his work on ordained ministry over the last decade as an instance of socio-historical polemicism. A once traditional theologian 'discovers' sociology and then uses it to relativize the foundations of sacerdotal priesthood. Caught up in the radicalism of the Dutch Catholic Church in the decades following Vatican II, Schillebeeckx has been unable to see that it is theology and not the social sciences which should underpin ordained ministry.

At first sight there might seem to be some justification for this view of Schillebeeckx. His initial analysis of ordained ministry had a somewhat polemical title, *Ministry: A Case for Change*,[1] and produced such controversy that it was soon followed by a revised version with a more eirenic title, *The Church with a Human Face*.[2] Further, its central argument, namely that the concept of sacerdotal priesthood can be traced back to the notion of *ordo* in the Roman empire, undoubtedly had a polemical edge, as the following extract indicates:

> In the Roman empire, *ordo* had the connotation of particular social classes differing in status. The senators formed the 'higher order', into which one would be 'instituted' (*in-ordinari* or *ordinari*). Under the Gracchi, an order of *equites* came into being between the *ordo senatorum* and the *plebs*, or the people (here *ordinari* then means becoming an *eques*); only later was the *plebs* itself also an *ordo*. Thus finally people talked of *ordo et plebs*, i.e. the upper, leading class, and the ordinary people, a terminology which not only introduced influence from the Old Testament but also coloured the difference between clergy and the people (laity): after the time of Constantine the church *ordinatio* or appointment to the 'order of office-bearers' clearly became more attractive because the clergy were seen as a more exalted class in the church in comparison with the more lowly 'believers'. The clericalization of the ministry had begun![3]

Schillebeeckx was clear that social factors should be taken seriously. At one point he argued that, 'in church history it is possible to recognize three views of the priest (which are partly socially conditioned): patristic, feudal or mediaeval, and modern'.[4] And at another he claimed that in the mediaeval period, 'the new conceptions of law, *ius*, and thus of jurisdiction, brought about a division between the power of ordination and the power of jurisdiction . . . lawyers developed the idea of "sacred power" (*sacra potestas*), strongly influenced by the context in which they lived'.[5]

Yet to ascribe all of this to social determinism would be seriously to misunderstand Schillebeeckx. Underlying all of his work is a deep commitment to the New Testament, and underlying his understanding of ordained ministry is a belief that contemporary forms of ministry need to recapture a perspective closer to the New Testament. Rather than viewing his use of socio-history as a polemical weapon, it might be more accurate to see it as a means whereby Schillebeeckx seeks to understand the discrepancy he has already discovered between New Testament and other notions of ministry. Confronted with evident pluralism, even within Dutch Catholicism, he uses a mixture of social scientific and historical research to understand why things are as they are. And that surely is one of the tasks for which the social sciences are well suited.

In very similar terms, the Canadian Catholic theologian Gregory Baum has described why he took a two-year leave of absence from teaching theology to study sociology:

> I was interested in sociology largely because I could not understand why the Catholic Church, despite the good will of clergy and laity and the extraordinary institutional event of Vatican II, had been unable to move and adopt the new style of Catholicism outlined in the conciliar documents. I thought that sociology, as the systematic enquiry of society, should be able to answer this question. But what I did not expect was the profound influence that the study of sociology would have on my entire theological thinking. I became convinced that the great sociological literature of the nineteenth and early twentieth centuries records human insights and human wisdom as much as philosophical writings, and that it ought to have a special place in the education of philosophers and theologians.[6]

As one of the foremost theologians to make a systematic use of sociology, Baum's opinion is instructive. He believes that a perception of pluralism and dissonance preceded his sustained sociological enquiries. As an observer of Vatican II and of the theological revolution that it signalled, he was aware that cognitive theology was not its only agenda. Indeed, there seemed to be an agenda in some ways far more powerful than cognition, but largely unacknowledged. Yet his subsequent publications also show that he is well aware of the methodological relativism that is implicit within sociology itself. He is conscious both of the attractiveness of many of the ideas and procedures within the discipline and also of their imperialistic tendencies. He remains a theologian, but one fully aware of the powers and pitfalls of a sociological perspective.

To return to Schillebeeckx, it is possible that the social tools that he uses are even sharper than he initially imagined. In *Ministry: A Case for Change* there are several moments of dissonance when Schillebeeckx appeared to be torn between his theological vision and the realities of the Catholic Church in which he remains a priest. So, he argued strongly that a link between ministry and community was essential within the New Testament and should act as a yardstick for ordained ministry today. Not surprisingly he expressed a dislike for private masses in the body of the text. There, having pointed out that the mediaeval notion was that a priest had 'power of the eucharist' and therefore could celebrate on his own, he stated bluntly, 'For the early church this was quite simply inconceivable.'[7]

Yet in a footnote the more traditional priest re-emerges: 'I am in no way denying the value of a private mass as deep personal prayer, much less its formative value for the priest who celebrates it; I am simply saying that in terms of the priestly ministry and the church, at least it is very peripheral.'[8]

For the sociologist to understand why Schillebeeckx writes as he does it is naturally important to know about his own social and personal context. Thus his use of the social sciences can legitimately be seen as both a response to the pluralism and dissonance that confronts him in contemporary Catholicism and as a symptom of his own dissonance. Further, in the increasingly ecumenical context of modern theology, Schillebeeckx's writings on ministry have themselves become a significant variable. If once they might simply have been a part of the internal debate within Catholicism, today they manifestly have wider significance. He has evidently been influenced by non-Catholic theologians – even though his outward style remains Catholic – and he in turn is widely read in non-Catholic circles. He thus becomes a direct contributant to the pluralism he observes and the socio-historical methods that he adopts soon become a means of relativizing his own hard-won conclusions. Paradoxically, the very method he adopts to understand and resolve dissonance becomes a potential source of further dissonance. Here is one of the most central challenges to theology today.

A very similar paradox confronts those New Testament scholars who have made an increasing, and increasingly imaginative, use of the social sciences.[9] In the last decade the literature in this area has grown enormously and shows no signs yet of slowing down. As I argued in chapter 3, it is becoming widely accepted that sociology is one of the tools that New Testament scholars must acquire. If initially there was some hesitation about subjecting New Testament texts to sociological methods – doubtless because of fears of reductionism – today it is difficult to avoid such methods altogether. The social context and social determinants of the New Testament are generally considered to be subjects of legitimate enquiry, by the theologically committed and uncommitted alike.

Yet this too has served to heighten the paradox of relativism. Nowhere is this more apparent than in biblical hermeneutics. Once it is observed that uses of the Bible are never neutral or impartial, but are directly related to the theological and ideological commitments of the users themselves, then relativism seems to follow. An observation of the circularity of hermeneutics soon suggests that there is not just one hermeneutical circle but an endless regression of hermeneutical circles. At its most cynical such a perspective concludes that the Bible is not a source of challenge or surprise but a cipher through which groups feed their ideological prejudices. The gibe that the Devil can quote scripture for his own purposes becomes pertinent for even the most sophisticated uses of the Bible.

This point can be illustrated historically. In the history of Christian attitudes towards participation in war the story of Jesus disarming Peter at Gethsemane often played a pivotal role.[10] For Tertullian it quite simply meant that Christians could not be soldiers. So in *On Idolatry* he argued as follows:

> Inquiry is made about this point, whether a believer may turn himself unto military service, and whether the military may be admitted unto the faith, even the rank and file, or each inferior grade, to whom there is no necessity for taking part in sacrifices or capital punishments. There is no agreement between the divine and the human sacrament, the standard of Christ and the standard of the devil, the camp of light and the camp of darkness. One soul cannot be due to two masters – God and Caesar. And yet Moses carried a rod, and Aaron wore a buckle, and John (Baptist) is girt with leather, and Joshua the son of Nun leads a line of march; and the people warred: if it pleases you to sport with the subject. But how will a Christian man war, nay, how will he serve even in peace, without a sword, which the Lord has taken away? For albeit soldiers had come unto John, and had received the formula of their rule; albeit, likewise, a centurion had believed; still the Lord afterward, in disarming Peter, unbelted ever soldier.[11]

But this interpretation of the story was starkly different from that advanced by Augustine two centuries later. In his *Reply to Faustus the Manichaean* Augustine used the story to argue that it was not the use of the sword but the unauthorized use of the sword which was forbidden by Jesus. Having rehearsed the story of Moses' act of violence, he concluded as follows:

> It was the same in Peter, when he took his sword out of its sheath to defend the Lord, and cut off the right ear of an assailant, when the Lord rebuked him with something like a threat, saying, 'Put up thy sword into its sheath; for he that taketh the sword shall perish by the sword' [Matt. 26.52–3]. To take the sword is to use weapons against a man's life, without the sanction of the constituted authority. The Lord, indeed, had told His disciples to

carry a sword; but He did not tell them to use it. But that after this sin Peter should become a pastor of the Church was no more improper than that Moses, after smiting the Egyptian, should become the leader of the congregation. In both cases the trespass originated not in inveterate cruelty, but in a hasty zeal which admitted of correction.[12]

And this interpretation was again starkly different from that of Aquinas in his *Summa Theologica*. For him, quite simply, 'the words, "Put your sword back in its scabbard" were directed to Peter as representing all bishops and clerics. Consequently, they may not fight.'[13]

Now, of course, it is perfectly possible to step outside academic hermeneutics and claim that one of these interpretations alone is correct. So a Christian pacifist might claim that Tertullian was correct in his understanding of the implications of this story, whereas Augustine had been corrupted by his post-Constantinian context and Aquinas by his mediaeval sacerdotal context. A Christian militarist, on the other hand, might claim that it was in fact Augustine who was correct, and that it was Tertullian, with his fear of surrounding Roman paganism, who had been corrupted. Characteristically either side has tended to use social explanations to explain the defects of opposing positions, whilst regarding their own position as immune from social determination (since it is actually true).

However, a more rigorously sociological perspective cannot adopt this ploy. None of the positions can be regarded as immune from social analysis and it is not at all difficult (from the perspective of the twentieth century) to trace the influence of their changing socio-political contexts upon their differing interpretations. Given Tertullian's sectarian tendencies and a socio-political context which he often regarded as profoundly alien, his thoroughgoing pacifist interpretation seems entirely predictable. Given the profound socio-political change in its status resulting from Constantine's (ambiguous) adoption of Christianity, it is again hardly surprising that first Ambrose and then Augustine wrestled with the theological possibility that wars could be both just and unjust and that Christians should participate fully in the former. And given the ontological division between clergy and laity that was so characteristic of the Middle Ages, and the centrality of papal rule and authority, it seems just as predictable that Aquinas should interpret a Petrine story as referring solely to the clergy.

But, of course, such sociological analysis can be used on all interpretations of this and every other biblical story. Indeed, the very process of subjecting biblical interpretation to sociological scrutiny heightens the paradox of relativism. A form of analysis, which at first offers attractive explanations of opposing interpretations, becomes a means of assessing all interpretations, including those currently cherished. It is not simply the liberalism of the nineteenth century which found its own face in the stories about Jesus, as Albert Schweitzer claimed. From the perspective of current research his own *Quest for the Historical Jesus* was itself culture-bound and socially located. And doubtless current research will appear similarly to future generations of scholars.

By openly recognizing the role of the interpreter in all biblical interpretation hermeneutics actually increases a sense of relativism. A particular hermeneutical perspective is explicitly adopted – feminist, liberationist, ethnic, or whatever – and then the Bible is interpreted accordingly. Yet it soon becomes obvious that there are a variety of (sometimes opposing) hermeneutical perspectives that could have been adopted and that the choice between them is socially bounded. Prejudgments (or, more cynically, prejudices) thus determine both the choice between perspectives and the manner and results of the subsequent biblical interpretation.

Again, once it is observed how frequently perspectives change within New Testament scholarship, a sense of relativism may also be heightened. The current interest in New Testament sociology appears as just that – a current interest. It is one amongst a number of ways of viewing the New Testament and it is one which has evoked varying reactions of suspicion or enthusiasm over the course of this century. It is currently in vogue and increasing, but may soon be supplanted by something else. But the 'something else' will hardly remove the problem. A greater methodological awareness may actually exacerbate the sense of relativism that is already so strong a by-product of sociological enquiry.

None of this is said to promote antagonism to New Testament sociology. On the contrary, I have argued elsewhere[14] that New Testament sociology is bringing fresh and illuminating insights into an area of scholarship which is prone to repetition. I remain an enthusiastic supporter, even whilst recognizing the heightened sense of relativism that it tends to induce. It is by no means the only source of this relativism. Structural changes in the way theology is taught – especially those involving ecumenical interaction – and the non-denominational horizons offered by religious studies (as distinct from theology) also induce a sense of relativism. If once it was possible to learn theology, even within universities, from a single denominational perspective, or even from the perspective of a single brand of churchmanship, today this is less common. Modern theology has become cross-fertilized and students tend to read eclectically across a variety of denominational perspectives. In the process they are inevitably confronted with considerable pluralism. Yet it is sociology which makes this pluralism abundantly manifest and it is sociology which encourages its users seemingly to undermine its own foundations.

Once sociology is adopted whole-heartedly it is free to turn back upon itself. So theologians who use sociology to inspect power and authority within the New Testament, need hardly be surprised if their own relationship to power and authority becomes an object of inspection by others. Liberation theology explicitly invites others to do this. New Testament sociology may be as yet less prepared. Certainly a sociological observation of New Testament sociologists suggests as much. There would appear to be presumptions and practices within the discipline which may tell others as much about their internal rivalries as about the material they are seeking to analyse.

A number of authors and works could be used to illustrate this, but two will have to suffice, Wayne Meeks' *The First Urban Christians: The Social World of the Apostle Paul*[15] and John Gager's *Kingdom and Community: The Social World of Early Christianity*.[16] Both works are a *tour de force* and, as a I argued earlier, two of the most able examples of New Testament sociology yet to emerge. Meeks was already known for his scholarly attempt to use the sociology of knowledge to understand the mixture of paradox and exclusivity in John's Gospel.[17] In *The First Urban Christians* he showed that he was able to use a wide range of sophisticated sociology to understand Paul. Gager, as noted in chapter 3, made an early and extensive use of the concept of cognitive dissonance from social psychology to illuminate the tensions of New Testament eschatology. Very obviously their work is the product more of religious studies than traditional theology.[18] They are relatively uninterested in the theological questions that are more typically asked by New Testament scholars working in theology departments or seminaries. Yet curiously both continue one of the most deeply held practices of New Testament scholars – the extensive citation of secondary sources.

The First Urban Christians contains altogether 299 pages of which only 192 are text. 36 pages are needed for the bibliography of secondary works cited. *Kingdom and Community* also contains a ratio of three pages of text to one page of notes. The crucial second chapter, entitled 'The End of Time and the Rise of Community', has 140 footnotes, occupying 9 pages. In terms of the practices of other New Testament scholars this is probably not at all exceptional. For a sociologist such detailed citation of secondary opinion might seem more unusual. It raises the interesting question, why are New Testament scholars so keen to cite secondary sources? And, why are they so concerned to say how many others agree or disagree with them?

Within much New Testament scholarship it is simply assumed that a scholarly work ought to contain detailed citations of secondary opinion. Yet curiously this practice is used both to endorse an opinion offered by the author and to show how many others got the matter wrong. The fact that others have all said something is thus not in itself used either to support or to refute a particular position. Rather multiple citation seems to be assumed to be a part of the proper presentation of scholarly material, and authors who reject this are notably defensive about doing so. Thus Graham Shaw's startling and deeply instructive *The Cost of Authority*, which is enticingly subtitled *Manipulation and Freedom in the New Testament*, begins with an extended apologia for its lack of footnotes and secondary citations:

> The slight reference in what follows to contemporary New Testament study does not imply indifference to that enterprise, far less any fundamentalist repudiation of it. It is rather that the questions with which this book is concerned have not received close attention, and those questions suggested a distinctive method of understanding the New Testament. Instead of defending this method by contrasting it with a more conventional approach, I thought it best simply to use the method and leave others to make the appropriate comparisons. I will be surprised if all my suggestions find ready agreement; but I hope that impatience with any particular conclusions will not obscure the importance of the questions I have raised and the necessity of devising some method to answer them.[19]

But of course he knew that they would. To be taken fully seriously by other New Testament scholars it is important, as Gager and Meeks are aware, not to flout their conventions. To offer both a startlingly different interpretation of well-known material and to flout such conventions is to risk the very impatience Shaw feared.

It is possible that multiple citation is a way of demonstrating scholarship in a discipline permanently threatened by relativism. New Testament scholarship has undergone so many changes over the course of this century and has been criticized so heavily by 'the faithful', that it would not be surprising if it showed evidence of insecurity. Since Christian faith is so often felt to depend upon its results and those results are themselves so fickle, it is a discipline which is both threatening and threatened. An extension of the discipline into religious studies – and away from denominational commitments – may not altogether eliminate this insecurity. Traces of it still seem to be present in New Testament sociology. And its own distinct relativism doubtless continues to feed it.

Amongst systematic theologians a knowledge of sociology and the relativism that it engenders is less common. In this respect the work of Stephen Sykes is a very important exception. In his *The Identity of Christianity* he shows that he is well aware of this central challenge to modern theology. For many years he has been concerned with the debate about the 'Essence of Christianity' initiated by Schleiermacher which he traces through Newman, Harnack, Troeltsch and Barth. In contrast to some of their positions he argues that conflict is actually inherent within Christianity. It is not simply that conflict has been variously present within the history of Christianity (as empirically it obviously has). Rather conflict is regarded as an abiding reality, which might be contained within parameters, but cannot ever be fully resolved. In contrast to Newman he argues:

> Not merely is conflict inherent in the early days of the Christian movement, it is inherent in the very existence of the Christian Church at every stage of its life. Moreover, in the case of the early Christian movement we argued that the ambiguities giving rise to many of the conflicts were not the result of deliberate misunderstanding or malice, but were the indirect consequence of carrying out Jesus' intentions in new contexts. Similarly in the later history of the Church, it may not be sheer bad faith, pride, or wilful disobedience which gives rise to disputes. Conflict arises because there is real difficulty in determining the proper relationship between the internal dimension of Christian commitment, and decisions or teaching about its diverse external dimensions.[20]

Sykes explicitly rejects ontological relativism, but is still aware of the methodological relativism implicit within this analysis of

Christianity. To resolve this dilemma he insists upon two key factors. The first of these involves the social function of theologians. For Sykes theologians have a key role in making sense of the obvious pluralism of Christianity and seeking to define its identity. This social function is not simply a cognitive enterprise (as it is usually thought to be by modern theologians), it also involves them in power within churches. So he argues:

> In a situation of internal conflict about the identity of Christian-ity . . . the necessary decisions are taken in the light of the clarification of the issues provided by theologians. Theologians are active across the entire range of dimensions of Christianity, from doctrines and ethics to ritual and social embodiment, because in each case a theological, or interpretative discipline has grown up in order to make meanings as precise as possible. Theologians are, therefore, necessarily involved in the internal power struggles which conflicts provoke . . . But theologians seem remarkably reluctant to expose their own activities to this disturbing analysis. They are happier, for obvious reasons, to write large and impressive works exploring the reasons why the traditional authorities are supposed to have collapsed, than to ask questions about the power which such books tacitly deliver to the theologian in the new situation.[21]

The second key factor which Sykes offers as a means of containing relativism is worship. Throughout his writings he has argued that worship is of central significance for theology. In *The Integrity of Anglicanism*[22] he argued that it is Anglican worship which gives Anglicanism, as pluralistic as it undoubtedly is, its integrity and theological identity. Despite all the many theological conflicts and disagreements within Anglicanism, it does have some unity in its worship. In *The Identity of Christianity* he takes this argument further to encompass synchronic and diachronic Christia-nity. He now argues that Christian identity is to be found in the interaction between its inward element and its external forms, and that it is worship which is central to this process of interaction. For Sykes 'worship itself contextualizes the activities of theologians'.[23] Worship contains both the internal element of experience of new life with the external forms of doctrines, myths and symbols. And 'participation in the communal worship of the Christian community fulfils the requirement of the internal element, namely that the heart of the believer also be engaged in the maintenance of Christian identity, by means of an inwardly appropriate sense of what needs to be achieved in the world. Thus the identity of Christianity consists in the interaction between its external forms and an inward element, constantly maintained by participation in communal worship.'[24]

Sykes is aware, of course, that Christian worship, and especially liturgical forms, vary synchronically and change diachronically. He is also aware that the nature of the interaction between an internal element and external forms, which constitutes for him the identity of Christianity, is itself elusive and difficult to codify. For this very reason he believes that conflict has an abiding and healthy role within Christian communities. Neither the social function of theologians nor the centrality of worship actually dissolve relativism. Rather they explicitly recognize that Christianity has a strong tendency to pluralism and could, without some form of social control, soon become fragmented and thoroughly relativized.

It is not necessary to adopt all of Sykes' terminology or conclusions to realize that he at least has taken the dilemma of relativism in modern theology seriously. His own exploration of sociology has led him to be more conscious of theologians as being themselves social agents (an insight that is still very rare). Using analyses of power relationships may well disturb fellow theologians and invite rejoinders to the effect that theology becomes an arbitrary pawn in some larger ecclesiastical game. Yet it does at least offer the possibility of a vision of theology as a social system which could present a more serious alternative to the competing convictions that have been analysed in previous chapters. It is to this possibility that I must turn in the final chapter.

8 · Theology – A Social System

This book has attempted to raise the challenge presented by viewing theology and the churches as socially and culturally relative. It is understandable that some in the theological world deny this relativity and seek doctrinal, biblical or ecclesiastical constants with which to refute it. Modern fundamentalism, in the various forms already studied, represents one of the most striking attempts to do this. However, it has been argued throughout that, from a sociological perspective, such attempts misunderstand the nature of modern pluralistic society. And, from a theological perspective, it has been argued that they distort faith by seeking to confine a relationship to specific propositions, doctrines, or practices.

The guiding concept in this chapter is that theology is a thoroughly relational discipline. It is relational in the sense in which Mannheim used the term.[1] All of its ideas and notions are socially rooted: the signs and symbols that theology uses have social antecedents and are mediated through specific social contexts: its methods and procedures relate to current and changeable social expectations: and its passing conclusions can have social roles and even effect changes in social structures. However theology is also relational in a second sense. Since it is *theo*logy and not *socio*logy it attempts to express, understand and interpret a relationship to God – and, for Christians, a relationship to God in Christ.

This second understanding of theology as relational does not invalidate the first, since every attempt to 'express, understand and interpret' a relationship to God is itself socially rooted and relative to specific social contexts. Even when certain signs and symbols apparently transcend relative social contexts, on account of their canonical, credal and/or liturgical status, their reception and interpretation are still socially relative. Like all relationships a relationship to God cannot adequately and without considerable distortion be reduced to words. But, as a relationship which is, in addition, diachronic, it cannot be expressed in the same words across radically different societies without even further distortion. An understanding of theology from the perspective of the sociology of knowledge assumes that theology is always a socially relative enterprise.

The present chapter will attempt to unpack some of the implications of this understanding of theology and then to suggest three models that might be developed responding to modern pluralistic society. Together these models outline a system. A proper elaboration of this system must wait for a later date. For the moment it is hoped that they might indicate that social and cultural relativity is not the theological enemy that at first it might seem. Relative convictions may not, after all, be absurd.

I

It is important to distinguish this relational understanding of theology from a purely reductionist understanding. Social reductionism has been commonplace both in theological polemics, as has been seen, and in positivist dismissals of theology and metaphysics. Both have tended to confuse methodology with ontology. So, in theological polemics, it has frequently been thought sufficient to show that opponents' views result from, or lead to, disreputable behaviour, or that these views have origins in particular, transient socio-political contexts. And in various versions of positivism it has often been imagined that it is sufficient to show that theistic beliefs can be explained without remainder in socio-psychological terms. But origins and validity should not be confused in this way and a method of social analysis should not be exalted into an ontology.

Mannheim, in contrast, was well aware that all views and ideas, one's own as well as those of one's opponents, can be analysed in social terms. If ideas are to be discredited simply because they are shown to be socially conditioned then one's own ideas appear equally vulnerable. Indeed, the sociology of knowledge is itself destroyed by its own axioms, since it is not difficult to relate the development of the discipline to particular socio-political factors. It was to avoid this obvious trap that Mannheim chose to use the term relationism. It avoided some of the connotations of the term relativism and the methodological confusions of reductionism.

Systematic theology then is not involved in reductionism in using Mannheim's relationism. On the contrary, it is recognizing that the extreme doctrinal, ethical and structural pluralism of Christianity is a correlate of the elusive theistic relationship upon which it is founded. If the foundation of Christianity was really a set of propositions, a cognitive revelation of some form, then this pluralism would be very confusing. It would be important to uncover the 'true' form of these propositions and to distinguish it from 'heretical' and distorted forms. The ecumenical task would consist of the heroic attempt to recover the cognitive foundation of Christianity hidden by the empirical pluralism of the historical and contemporary churches. If ecumenism has sometimes been seen in these terms its fruits have been very meagre. But if, in contrast, Christianity is seen as a form of religion founded upon an elusive relationship to God in Christ, then pluralism resulting from a myriad of socio-political contexts will be readily expected. And the consequent pluralism of Christian theology will also be readily expected.

By seeing theology as a relational discipline the theologian is recognizing both its historical contingency and its common foundation in a theistic relationship. All churches will, of course, attempt to set boundaries to guard against this contingency and will, as a result, risk confusing these boundaries with the theistic relationship itself. Boundaries – whether canonical, credal, pontifical or liturgical – are in some form essential to the identity of particular religious organizations. If a religious organization is to survive beyond an initial, fragile cultic phase, it must necessarily set structural and cognitive boundaries which distinguish it from the world at large. Churches, as religious organizations, are subject to these identity/ survival pressures and, as was seen in the previous chapter, an analysis of them in these terms is proving to be increasingly important for theologians as well as sociologists.

Whilst recognizing the unavoidability of these pressures, a relational understanding of theology will view their products as socially contingent. Empirically, there is no agreement amongst churches about which are or are not the essential boundaries. Pluralism within Christianity at this point is only too evident and Christian identities are manifestly varied. Theoretically, a relational understanding of theology would not expect the situation to be otherwise. It would expect boundary maintenance to be a socially relative phenomenon. From this perspective, boundary maintenance appears simultaneously as essential but as essentially contingent.

A fully relational understanding of theology contains just one non-contingent element, the theistic relationship. Despite the claims of some phenomenologists, there need be no claim here that humanity shares a common 'experience' of God, or even that Christians share a common 'experience' of God in Christ. The only socially accessible reports of religious 'experiences' take the form of historically contingent words. The latter suggests that pluralism may be as rife here as it is in all other aspects of religiosity. And, even within Christianity, reports appear highly varied. Of course it is still possible that, despite the varying reports, there is a common 'experience', either amongst humanity as a whole or amongst Christians, which is simply reported in historically contingent ways. This possibility can never be totally discredited, but it may seem more likely that a relationship to God, like other more mundane relationships, can be experienced in a variety of ways.

In any case a relational understanding of theology needs to assume only a common relationship. It makes this assumption simply because it is *theo*logy: theology is precisely that discipline which assumes the existence of a *theos* and then seeks to understand the cognitive, social and physical world as it relates to this *theos*.

Of course this assumption does not 'prove' or demonstrate the existence of God. Questions about the existence of God may belong properly to the philosophy of religion and not to theology at all. And they certainly do not belong to a relational understanding of theology. In fact, the latter may be highly critical of the whole philosophical enterprise of trying to establish the existence or non-existence of God. Viewed from the perspective of the sociology of knowledge, this enterprise makes the unsubstantiated assumption that there are non-contingent methods for establishing such issues. It assumes that philosophers can somehow step aside from their own social conditioning and arbitrate on matters of existence or non-existence. Whereas, viewed sociologically, philosophy itself appears as a contingent discipline subject to the social conventions and assumptions of society at large. Changes in philosophical ethos encourage the view that philosophy is not some independent arbiter but a part of the socio-cultural process of a given age.

Whether or not it entirely accords with the social conventions and assumptions of the age in which it is set, theology is precisely that discipline which treats the existence of God as axiomatic. Like all axioms this constitutes a point of departure and is only abandoned by stepping outside the discipline. For the theologian the question is whether the theistic axiom can generate insights for the rest of life.

If the theologian *qua* theologian treats the theistic relationship as axiomatic, the Christian theologian treats it as axiomatic that this relationship is to be located 'in Christ'. Again, when this christocentric relationship is expressed in words, when it is interpreted, or when its implications are specified, considerable pluralism is evident within Christianity.[2] For some, christocentrism implies a particularist understanding of other religious traditions: for others not. For some it is the 'historical' figure of Jesus discernible in the Synoptic Gospels which is the focus of their christocentrism: for others, like Paul, this historical figure plays a very minor role. For some, christocentrism excludes the theistic relationship being linked directly or indirectly with others in worship: for others, marian and dulian features are central to their liturgies.

In this context the term 'in Christ' simply locates a relationship and does not denote any particular understanding of this relationship. It is used to signify the specific theistic relationship that Christians have in common. Just as for theologians in general it is axiomatic that God exists, so for Christian theologians it is axiomatic that Christ is central to a relationship to God.

By regarding christocentrism as axiomatic to Christian theology, apologetics is seen as distinct from theology. Again the sociology of knowledge suggests scepticism about whether it is really possible to step outside religious traditions in order to assess their relative merits. Comparative religion was sometimes viewed in this way, as the discipline which is able to evaluate differing religions and to demonstrate the supremacy of one of them (usually Christianity). And, at the level of the individual, evangelism has sometimes been seen as the attempt to convert the 'outsider' through rational argument. In both cases christocentrism is not regarded as axiomatic but becomes the object of demonstration.

Without denying that individuals do make religious changes (they obviously do), a sociological approach would rather view these changes in context: cognitive changes would be set alongside possible structural changes. On this understanding, conversion is seen as a social, and not simply as a cognitive, process. In any case, just as philosophy cannot be viewed satisfactorily as a socially independent arbiter of 'truth', neither can apologetics, nor this old-style comparative religion, be seen as such independent arbiters. In recent religious studies there is now widespread recognition that this is the case. Although the term 'comparative religion' curiously still survives, it seldom carries the connotation of religious contestation. Rather it is widely accepted that cognitive comparisons across religious traditions can distort an adequate understanding of any of them. By accepting that religious traditions are best understood from within, and that cognitive comparisons across traditions tend to distort, the religious studies specialist is implicitly accepting a sociology of knowledge perspective. And viewed in terms of this perspective, christocentrism appears as a given of the Christian tradition (i.e. an axiom) and not as a position which can be independently verified.

II

Christian theology, then, is viewed by definition as both theistic and christocentric. It is theistic because it is *theo*logy and it is christocentric because it is *Christ*ian. Viewed in relational terms, it is seen as the product of a highly pluralist collection of communities and traditions (a pluralism which is both synchronic as well as diachronic) united only by a common location of a theistic relationship in Christ. And the*ology* is the ordered study of biblical, credal, liturgical and mystical expressions of this theistic relationship. It becomes systematic theology when it combines this ordered study with a strong interest in method and system. By convention, Christian systematic theology is identified as that type of theology which contains both a self-conscious method and an attempt to relate Christian expressions of faith to the three dominant themes of creation, redemption and sanctification. Together these three themes have supplied the framework for attempts to write systematic theology. If the sociology of knowledge supplies the overall method, the three themes will supply this framework for the system.

It should be stressed that this framework is a convention and that the method is certainly not the only way to approach systematic theology. Nonetheless, I hope to show that this method does yield fruitful insights and that the framework is peculiarly appropriate. Viewed from the perspective of the sociology of knowledge, the theme of creation particularly involves the study of the social context of theology, whereas that of redemption involves more the study of the social determinants of theology, and that of sanctification that of the study of the social consequences of theology. Taken together these three modes of studying theology offer an overall view of theology as a social system.

Another way of understanding these three modes is to see them as three distinct but interconnected ways of studying the relation between religion and society. If the first is primarily concerned with expressions of religion to be found in the natural order of creation, the second is concerned with the process of religious socialization through which distinctive soteriological positions are formed, and the third with the way these positions once formed in religious communities can in turn shape society. Or to express this more technically, the first is concerned mostly with religion as an implicit variable, the second with religion as a dependent variable, and the third with religion as an independent variable.

Although analytically distinct these three sets of variables are clearly also interconnected. Even if religion is viewed as an implicit variable it should not be viewed sociologically as *sui generis*. Some phenomenologists might wish to insist that it is, but the sociologist is methodologically inclined always to seek further social ante-cedents. Given the long and complex history of religious symbols and the varying fluctuations of religious organizations, a judgment of *sui generis* should perhaps not be made too readily. Instead the implicit religion of today might more appropriately be seen as the remnants of an explicit and influential religion of the past (it is this observation which *mutatis mutandis* makes natural law claims so problematic for the sociologist). Once accepted, the link between the three sets of variables, and the three modes of study that they represent, can at once be seen. Implicit variables derive from prior independent variables and these in turn have been moulded as dependent variables. Theological models seen as social models are always subject to this three-way process.

Using a method derived initially from the sociology of knowledge and working within the conventional three-fold framework of creation, redemption and sanctification, three theological models might be developed. It is essential that these models relate to present-day, pluralistic Western society, since this is the social context in which they are to function. There is perhaps a growing awareness amongst theologians that theological models do need to be culturally specific. If once it was assumed that Western theolog-ical models could be transposed unchanged into Third-World countries, today it is more often realized that countries need to develop their own models which relate more clearly to their own social contexts.

Liberation theology has been particularly successful in demon-strating to Western theologians that this is the case. Derived not from the comparative affluence of Western mixed economies but from situations of real poverty and inequality of economic and political distribution, liberation theology has achieved a distinc-tively non-Western voice. It also provides a very obvious example of theology acting as an implicit, dependent and finally indepen-dent, social variable.[3] But, despite some attempts to transpose it into the Western context, it is primarily a Third-World and not a

Western theological model. It is designed to meet the needs of a situation of radical poverty and inequality and not the comparative affluence and egalitarianism of the West. It is meant to speak to and to change a people lacking a serious political voice and not those who can already be a party to changes through political ballots. From the perspective of the sociology of knowledge, it might appear to be just as inappropriate to transpose the model of liberation theology unchanged from a Third-World to a Western context as once it was to transpose Western models unchanged into Third-World contexts. It would amount to a curious imitation of missionary practices that are now rejected by the very proponents of liberation theology. In seeking models that relate to the specifically Western situation, the Western theologian is adopting the same procedure, but not the same models, as the liberation theologian.

On this understanding, it is the function of models to act as culturally specific mediators. Models, whether scientific, social scientific or theological, may be seen as everyday concepts or entities used obliquely to denote and make present realities which cannot be described adequately in univocal terms. As Max Black insisted,[4] models are not props for feeble minds, mere pictures or illustrations whose meaning could be abstracted into literal terms. They are irreducible precisely because the realities they denote cannot, without serious distortion, be described literally. For Black they are good models in so far as they are speculative instruments which lead their users to see new connections. The abandonment of picturability in higher physics necessarily involves a view of reality which can be known only obliquely and through contingent means. In this respect it corresponds more closely than was once supposed with the world of the theologian.[5] Both are concerned with developing insights through the use of models which cannot properly be reduced to literal terms just because their object cannot be so reduced. And both are subject to the constraints of the social context for and from which they develop their models.

III

In looking to the natural order, models of creation raise particular problems for twentieth-century Westerners. In the comparatively monolithic social world of thirteenth-century Christendom it could more readily be assumed that the natural order was naturally ordered. From this natural order people could discern natural law and through purely rational means they could establish both the existence of, and even some of the attributes of, the Creator.[6] If some were unable to make such discernments, this could be ascribed to bad social customs or individual perversity. It certainly was not seen as decisive evidence against the existence of natural law. Even the major confrontations between Christendom and Islam, or the continuing presence of Jewish and sectarian minorities within Christendom, were not sufficient to undermine this sense of natural order. Even very considerable moral diversity amongst 'others' need not conflict with a belief in natural law, provided such diversity is seen as the product of individual or social perversity. In all of this there is a clear link between political hegemony, social and ecclesiastical order, and confidence in the natural order. So, even if it could be shown that Aquinas was mistaken in some of his assumptions about the natural order (e.g. in his understanding of women or slaves), there still could be overall confidence, both that there is a natural order, and that its properties can be established through the use of reason.

Natural law assumptions are still apparent in the West today – as the resurgence of language about 'rights' indicates – but they have lost much of their social support. It might be argued that the present-day West is characterized less by confidence in political, social and natural order, than by pluralism and diversity. This pluralism has several sources within the West. It may in part be the product of democratic political decision-making: political order is not imposed from above but is the self-conscious product of the people and is thus subject to their changeable desires. It may in part be a consequence of what Berger terms 'modernity', itself the product of information technology, increased mobility, and rapid urbanization.[7]

The contrast between 'modernity' and traditional society can be made too starkly, and the degree to which Westerners have serious 'choices' in their lives can be exaggerated. Nonetheless, pluralistic modernity does have obvious applicability to Western society and provides a clear contrast with the competing convictions of the Victorian churches. Pluralism may even be a part product of, or at the very least a symptom of, denominationalization and possibly ecumenism. If the notion of the natural order was once fostered and supported by the mediaeval Catholic Church (both as a system of meaning and as a system of control), ecclesiastical diversity may tend to undermine this, especially if this diversity is viewed (ecumenically) in the inclusive terms of denominationalism. The exclusivism and absolutism of either the universal church or the radical sect are more conducive to the claims of individual or social perversity that must be used to protect natural law against the evidence of moral diversity. The inclusive denomination, as will be apparent from earlier chapters, is today less likely to view its own understanding of the natural order as *the* understanding of this order, and then to seek to protect this understanding by anathematizing others. As a result, excommunication, once so frequent in Presbyterian congregations (as was seen in chapter 5), today becomes newsworthy because of its very rarity. The excommunication of an elder (however distinguished) by the Free Presbyterian Church of Scotland for attending Catholic requiem masses might once have appeared quite normal.

If natural law claims have increasingly become socially less plausible, traces of 'orderliness' can nevertheless still be found within twentieth-century Western culture. Within the moral sphere this is most evident in the phenomenon of moral outrage. Despite the obvious diversity of moral view-points and despite a wide-spread belief that these view-points are at best tentative and socially relative, there is still considerable evidence that many (perhaps most) feel deep moral outrage at instances of cruelty to children, sexual abuse of women, famine in the Third World, ecological pollution, etc. Indeed, voluntary charities concerned with such issues largely depend in their appeals for contributions upon being able to evoke moral outrage in the public at large. Hence their appeals are made more through the deliberate use of pictures illustrating cruelty to children (etc.) than through the deployment of sustained rational argument.

Strangely, the negative phenomenon of moral outrage is asymmetrically related to positive expressions of moral commitment in the West today. If the latter appear tentative, optional and frequently confused, the former appears passionate, obligatory and surprisingly unified. Of course synchronic diversity can be found within contemporary expressions of moral outrage and diachronic diversity can be seen from the fact that not all objects of moral outrage have remained constant (slavery has not always been such an object). Further, individuals can be found who apparently have no sense of moral outrage, although, instructively, Western societies tend to label them as psychopaths. Yet, having made these important concessions (concessions which would be damaging to a throroughgoing natural law theory), a remarkable asymmetry remains. Moral outrage suggests an 'orderliness' belied by expressions of moral diversity.

The term 'orderliness' is perhaps too confusing in this context. It is too close to the model of 'order' present in theories of natural order and natural law and thus may belong more to the juridical hegemony of the thirteenth century than to the pluralism of the West today. 'Givenness', on the other hand, avoids some of these overtones. It can at times be used to signify fixity and unchangeability, but this is not its primary signification. If order is frequently imposed, gifts more usually denote a dynamic relationship. If orderliness suggests a world in equilibrium sustained by rationality, givenness suggests a less predictable, relational world in which equilibrium cannot be presupposed. If order can be imposed through rewards and punishments, gifts are more usually the products of affectionate relationships and lack the strict reciprocity of rewards. Finally, to claim that the world shows signs of 'orderliness' suggests a grand-design which more modest claims for signs of 'givenness' eschew.

Viewed from the perspective of a model of givenness, the phenomenon of moral outrage appears as anger directed, less at an order that has been disturbed, than at a gift that has been rejected and perhaps destroyed. So, cruelty to children offends, not so much because it disrupts an imposed order (or even the self-imposed order of utilitarianism), but because it maltreats life which is a gift (children themselves). In terms of this model, children are seen as gifts to be received with gratitude and not as objects to be subdued and abused at will. The utilitarian would suggest that such an attitude results from a calculation of what is ultimately in our own interests as social beings. But in practice, moral outrage at cruelty to children is seldom calculated and can readily be evoked in people not remotely connected with the victims (as Oxfam has often shown). Further, action directed against the objects of moral outrage frequently militates against the very calculated order presupposed by utilitarians, particularly if the victims belong to despised minorities.

The model of givenness is also relevant to a number of different positive ethical theories. Deontological theories of ethics all tend to manifest signs of givenness. Being based upon a strong sense of moral imperative which disregards consequences, they are more closely related to 'gifts' than to 'rewards'. For them the 'ought' and the 'good' are given, both in the sense that they exist independently of rational calculation, and in the sense that they make claims upon the individual. In the language of rights and correlative duties this becomes very evident: rights are given to individuals and individuals, in most cases at least, have correlative duties. However, even consequentialist theories of ethics are not without elements of givenness, since individuals are enjoined to consider the consequences of their actions upon others even when personal repercussions are extremely remote. If an individual does not at the very least accept the principle of universalizability in ethics, most ethical theories cannot function. The determinedly selfish individual is a problem even for utilitarianism: some respect for others seems to be a minimum requirement of ethical theory.

The model is also relevant to a number of other areas of present-day Western culture. The term *data* still survives within science: indeed, language about the natural world is still surprisingly personalist. In addition, most scientists proceed on the assumption that the world is inherently intelligible and not on the assumption (as the sociology of science would suggest) that the intelligibility of the natural world is a human construct. They even, at times, display awe and wonder at the natural world, particularly at its macroscopic and microscopic levels. None of this accords with the view of science forwarded by the logical positivists. Rather it conforms more closely to the language suggested by the model of givenness.

Again, the creative arts are redolent with suggestions of givenness. It is commonplace, even within the twentieth century, for artists, composers and authors to talk about 'inspiration' and to use language which suggests that they are recipients of 'gifts'. Many of them characteristically have periods of inactivity and frustration when they feel that they must wait for 'inspiration' to return and, when it does, feel surprise and 'otherness' in the presence of the product of their creation. It is commonplace to talk of performers and intellectuals of any sort as 'gifted', language suggesting that ability is a gift rather than a reward, and an object of gratitude and response rather than *hubris* and conceit. The moral overtones are clear. But connotations of 'otherness' and external personalism are also suggested.

All of this can be contained in a purely sociological frame. Connotations of 'givenness' and 'otherness' can be interpreted sociologically as survivals of a once religious age, religious terms transposed into a secular context. The caring professions offer many examples of such transpositions. The once clerical notions of vocation, confessional secrecy, absolution and salvation now find secular counterparts in notions of professional vocation, confidentiality, treatment and health. Professions even have their codes, orthodoxies, and procedures for exclusion/excommunication. Yet only those who are otherwise religious may be impressed by the transcendent connotations of these secular transpositions. For the secular they remain secular, despite their religious ancestry. Like Comte, they can argue that specifically religious interpretations of social phenomena constitute a passing and past phase through which culture develops. From this perspective, science, or social science, offer more plausible frames for people today.

The theologian, on the other hand, views the world differently. Precisely because theology seeks to express, interpret and understand the cognitive, social and physical world as it relates to God, it finds connotations of 'givenness' and 'otherness' in the secular realm irresistible. A relational theology, which seeks to use the sociology of knowledge, will not be tempted to imagine that such connotations invalidate the sociological enterprise, let alone provide independent evidence for the existence of God. Rather, because it is relational also in a theistic sense, it views these connotations as consonant with its own implicit theism. Of course, the whole of life is properly the object of theology, and not simply those parts which prompt religious imagery. Nonetheless, a theology which seeks to respond to social context legitimately pays particular attention to the latter. Social phenomena which act as such prompters are not thereby hypostasized, as if they are unchanging features of every age and society. Rather, fully recognized as socially relative phenomena, they become temporary prompters for theologians of a relationship to God which transcends mundane relativism.

For the theologian language about 'givenness' and 'gifts' irresistibly implies a 'giver'. *Data* becomes *adeodata* (the term, in its masculine singular form, that the 'pagan' Augustine instructively used to name his son). Life is seen not simply as 'given' but as 'God-given'. And 'gifts' within life are believed to require, not just humility in the presence of something unearned, but also gratitude to the divine giver. To the moral response, which the theologian shares with the secularist, is added prayerful thanksgiving and doxology. The difference between *data* and *adeodata*, then, is less a moral difference than a referential and attitudinal difference. References to the source of *data* affect attitudes to *data*, even though a recognition of *data* as *data* already makes some moral responses more appropriate than others. Thus, if humility is required by both *data* and *adeodata*, worship springs rather from an identification of *data* as *adeodata*. In this, morality unites, but worship differentiates.

An adeodatic model can also serve to reinforce and strengthen a secular understanding. If, in secular terms, moral outrage is seen as anger that a gift has been rejected and perhaps destroyed, in theological terms it may be seen as a rejection of both the gift and the giver. Abuse of children, women, the poor, or the environment, are seen as abuse of divine gifts. Gifts of intelligence or creativity that are unused are seen as rejected divine gifts. And moral imperatives that are recognized as moral imperatives, but are still unheeded, appear as God-given imperatives that are disobeyed.

The continuities between natural and divine that are essential to traditional natural law theory pertain here, even if the juridical frame does not. Grace crowns nature: *adeodata* reinforces and supplements *data*. It reinforces *data* by grounding it in a theistic relationship: it supplements it by identifying the giver and not the given as the object of devotion. Life identified in adeodatic terms is neither sacred nor profane. It is not in itself sacred since it is identified as a part of creation: but neither is it entirely profane since it is identified as a gift of the creator and not simply as a product of creation.

Taken on its own, however, an adeodatic model is vulnerable. Gifts can be irresponsible, irrational and the vehicles of only transitory affections. Irresponsible gifts can serve to de-skill their recipients, as relief agencies know only too well. Irrational gifts can confuse and de-stabilize, as can gifts that are not derived from relationships of sustained love and care. Social anthropologists have sometimes pointed to the semantic link in German between 'gifts' and 'poison'.[8] In face-to-face peasant communities gifts have important, and sometimes sinister, connections with status and control. Giving, in itself, is not always virtuous and gift-relation-ships range from the functional to the intimate. If some sociologists have seen gift-relationships as evidence of unexpectedly altruistic behaviour,[9] others, particularly in developmental sociology, appear more suspicious. *A fortiori*, givenness as a theological model is also susceptible to ambiguity. A creator who gives at whim might even appear demonic.

A traditional theory of natural order could cope with this problem in a way that an adeodatic model cannot. Order militates against whim and teleological arguments could be advanced as evidence of this order and as evidence of God as the orderer. Purpose was seen as present within the natural order and all those capable of rational inspection could be expected to be able to perceive this. The order and the orderer alike were viewed as eminently rational and responsible, and the relationship between creature and creator could be set out schematically in terms of rewards and punishments.

In regarding this whole frame as less plausible today, an adeodatic model clearly re-introduces the problem which the frame effectively resolved in the past. Order is no longer presupposed: creation is regarded as too ambiguous to sustain teleological arguments; and a system of rewards and punishments is viewed as too juridical and paternalistic. Despite the claims of some eminent sociologists,[10] a reward-compensation model in the sociology of religion may be too simplistic to account for religious belonging in late twentieth-century Western societies. To a theologian it appears even more simplistic.

IV

An adeodatic model clearly cannot function alone in any sustainable religious tradition. It is to be found in a number of traditions – most obviously in the monotheistic traditions of Judaism, Christianity and Islam, but also in some of the Bakti traditions of India – yet it is seldom found alone. It is usually combined with other models. It is a feature of all of these traditions that the relationship of God to the world is never captured in a single model. The very nature of religious language necessarily precludes this. If it is a function of all models, whether scientific, social scientific, or theological, that they seek to denote realities which cannot, without serious distortion, be described literally, then it would seem improbable that this could ever be achieved through the use of a single model. In theology the reality to be denoted is so patently irreducible that the prospect of any single model being able to achieve this is not probable at all. All of these religious traditions recognize this in the bewildering range of models that they present to their adherents. In the case of the adeodatic model there are also the above logical reasons for considering that on its own it is not a sufficient model to denote the theistic relationship. Further, the framework offered by systematic theology requires other models to denote the themes of redemption and sanctification.

The theme of redemption is particularly concerned with religious identity. If creation is regarded as inherently ambiguous, religious traditions can be seen as attempts to overcome this ambiguity. They insist upon some special revelation – which in Christianity focusses upon christology – as a means of reducing or resolving ambiguity and of thus coping with pluralism. Viewed sociologically this will inevitably appear as projection, but viewed theologically it appears rather as the re-interpretation of secular experience in terms of the boundaries of a faith tradition. A pattern is imposed on natural discernments of the 'given': *data*, even *adeodata*, becomes teleological *data*.

If a traditional theory of natural order tended to locate teleology within the realm of natural experience, and even used it as a plank within apologetics, a relational approach locates teleology instead within a faith tradition. Teleology is now seen more as an expression of faith than as a means to faith; it is an interpretation of natural experience rather than issuing out of this experience; it is fostered through religious socialization rather than acting as a prelude to this socialization; it is a theological elaboration (though not, on that account, a theological fabrication) rather than a theological given. And, in a relational theology within the Christian tradition, it is linked more appropriately with christology than with the theme of creation.

The *Logos* tradition in Christianity most clearly expresses this link between teleology and christology. In the Johannine prelude the *Logos* is indeed linked with creation and is now made manifest in Jesus, but only to those who have eyes to see this. The fact that the *Logos* is involved in creation does not mean that everyone can naturally discern it – it is hidden teleology that is revealed in Jesus. The English translation of *logos* as 'word' does scant justice to this teleological dimension: the Greek also has connotations of 'purpose' and 'rationality'. 'Purposiveness' perhaps denotes this better: 'God's purposiveness became flesh; he came to dwell among us' (perhaps even, 'In the beginning was Logic . . .').

A similar link between teleology and christology is also apparent in the prelude of Ephesians; God 'has made known to us his hidden purpose – such was his will and pleasure determined beforehand in Christ'. Again, the central model of the Kingdom of God in the Synoptics has both christological and teleological links. In the Synoptics, Jesus has a unique relationship to God's kingly rule: it is inaugurated through him, and his parables and miracles are related to it at almost every point. For the Synoptics, Jesus' relationship to this rule is crucial for understanding his christological import. Further, the fact that the rule is sometimes present and sometimes future clearly implies that it is directional and teleological. Through this dominant Synoptic model, God's purposeful activity in the world is firmly related to the person and ministry of Jesus.

To use a model of 'purposiveness', then, to denote the theme of redemption is clearly within the boundaries of Christian tradition, and indeed goes back to the very earliest parts of this tradition. If, later, teleology was used rather to denote the theme of creation, this was understandable given the mediaeval concept of natural order, with its obvious socio-political as well as theological connections. Today, however, the earlier link may be more apposite.

It is even possible that present-day Western pluralism has some affinities with the religious pluralism within which earliest Christianity (especially in its urban Pauline form) sought to survive. In both instances exclusivist sectarianism offers an obvious means of survival. The New Testament offers many examples of this: it is arguably one of the features that differentiates John's Gospel from the Synoptics. From the perspective offered by the sociology of knowledge, exclusivist boundary maintenance is to be expected in a movement (whether religious or not) which is attempting to establish its identity. Viewed in these terms, it is the inclusivist positions in the New Testament which must appear the more remarkable. So, although Paul's christology/soteriology is predominantly exclusivist, it does have some remarkably inclusivist elements (e.g. in his understanding of the Patriarchs). The various links that the New Testament makes between teleology and christology are themselves divided on the exclusivist/inclusivist issue. They are united by the fact that they are all christocentric, but only some are christo-monopolistic. An important strand within the Christian tradition has always maintained that, although God's purposiveness is uniquely present in Jesus, this does not preclude the possibility that it can also be known in other religious traditions.

Exclusivist boundary maintenance may also be expected in parts of a, now ancient, religious tradition that is seeking to maintain identity confronted with modern pluralism. Nonetheless, the tradition itself still contains elements of inclusivism, and, to confuse matters further, has itself become increasingly pluralistic (thus making appeals to exclusive boundaries, such as those of the forms of fundamentalism discussed in earlier chapters, ever more difficult to sustain credibly). Without itself opting for an exclusivist position, a christological model of purposiveness consciously responds to contemporary pluralism, offering a path (but not necessarily the only path) through the ambiguities of present-day experience.

That, in itself, however, is an activity of limited usefulness. Most theistic religious traditions do not simply wish to provide an identity for their adherents: they wish, in addition, to mould society at large. Again, this is a point that reward-compensation theories of religious belonging tend to miss. A fully *socio*logical approach to religion rests uneasily with a mode of explanation concerned solely with individual identity. Similarly, a pietistic theological approach concerned only with individual salvation ignores the relationship of churches to societies at large.

This is perhaps one of the reasons why systematic theology has tended to contain the social themes of ecclesiology and eschatology within the broad ambit of sanctification. For the sociologist the theme of sanctification raises the issue of whether or not religion is an independent social variable. For the theologian it represents the outpouring of the Spirit into the world at large, the Kingdom of God transforming a secular world, and the world brought to an eschaton.

There can be little doubt that one of the most powerful Christian models to express this is that of *agape*. Not all ages in the past have seen *agape* as the central Christian virtue, that is as the virtue above all others that individual Christians and corporate churches ought (and often fail) to be manifesting in the world, and thereby transforming that world. However, in the West today it is seen as the central virtue. Perhaps for parts of the Third World 'liberation' is fast becoming the dominant model, but not within the West. Adopting *agape* as the third model recognizes both the popular perception of Christianity's central virtue and the degree to which this perception is itself culturally constrained, unaware, as it is, of the full depth of the model of *agape* within the New Testament.

Popular perceptions of *agape* present relational theology with a paradox. Some of the sharpest criticisms of Christianity today are manifestly based upon transposed Christian values. This point is more specific than the general claim that is sometimes made to the effect that the seeds of secularization lie within the Judaeo–Christian tradition itself. Rather it is evident in attacks on Christianity (usually as represented by the churches) for not living up to its own values, when the very attacks themselves presuppose these values. This is evident, for example, in the paradoxical way the medical profession is often loathe to treat clergy as recipients of confidentiality; in the way politicians are frequently hostile to church 'interventions' even on moral issues; and in the widespread belief that 'religion' is responsible for conflict and wars in the world today. In terms corresponding more closely to *agape*, these examples depend upon the prior beliefs; that it is doctors themselves who are the prime carers and the most reliable guardians of confidentiality; that it is politicians who can be trusted to care for society, even in specifically moral areas; and that it is commonsense, not religious socialization, which will foster a more caring and peaceful world.

At a sociological level, all of this presents considerable evidence that religious values may successfully be transposed into a secular context and then be regarded simply as secular values. At a theological level, it raises a number of important issues. There is evidently something uncontrollable about *agape*. Philosophers of religion frequently comment that 'love' is not susceptible to careful definition and that theological attempts to distinguish between *agape*, *eros* and *philia* often lack clarity or consistency. For the theologian, however, the problem is deeper than that: the claims of *agape* appear simultaneously as imperative but disruptive of order and system, especially when *agape* becomes a vehicle of self-criticism. Further, the theologian may be concerned about the roots and durability of values once removed from their theo*logical* setting.

In several parts of the New Testament there is a very intimate connection between *agape* as a moral value and *agape* as a theistic model. This relationship is most fully articulated in the Johannine Epistles. Quite remarkably, in a single verse (I John 4.7) *agape* is used first as a form of Christian address, then as a moral value, then as a theistic model, and finally as a means of expressing the ideal creature-creator relationship. The theo*logic* in the Epistles is clear: God may be depicted in terms of *agape*; God's relationship to humanity may also be depicted in terms of *agape*; so our relationship to God, and derivatively our relationship to each other, should also reflect *agape*. And in the Synoptics, a triadic relationship of *agape* is required in the dominical commands (God, neighbour, and then self), and it is *agape* which must be shown to enemies.

In Paul's writings it is *agape* which inspires his most lyrical theology and introduces an uncontrollable, and finally eschato-logical, feature. After all the rudeness of the earlier chapters of I Corinthians, chapter thirteen still appears remarkable, not least in the way that the apostle of faith presents the primacy of *agape*. He even highlights this primacy by the very position that he places the term *agape* in the various sentences (especially v. 13). This is evident, too, in the great eschatological crescendo of Romans (8.31–9): here *agape* is *the* model to denote our final relationship to God in Christ. For Paul, *agape* is manifestly very much more than a moral value: it has primacy (despite its uncontrollable features), it is a theistic model, and it is eschatological.

Using the model of *agape* to denote the theme of sanctification, two separate but related issues must be explored. The first of these concerns the way *agape* is incorporated within existing churches. Because it is an ideal or eschatological model the temptation to exaggerate the holiness of existing churches is more easily avoided. It is one of the oddest features of ecumenical dialogue that it often makes such exaggerations. In this dialogue, churches become paradigms of the new humanity in which divisions between class, sex and race are broken down and peace and fraternity pertain.[11] Further, and just as anomalously, churches are presented as having consistent and distinct theological positions over a range of doctrinal and moral issues.[12] A more sociological approach at this point might raise strong suspicions about such claims. However, it is also a function of the theological model of *agape* to raise such suspicions: the uncontrollable, eschatological and ideal-typical features of this model present existing churches with both a *telos* and a judgment on existing structures.

The second issue concerns the relation of *agape*, mediated through Chrisian traditions and structures, to the world at large. Again *agape* has both positive and negative functions. Positively, it seeks to re-interpret and mould the traces of secular 'givenness' noted earlier. Moral outrage, in particular, can be seen as a recognition that the given has been distorted, but it might further be seen as a recognition of *agape* affronted and denied. *Agape* demands the kind of altruism and selflessness ultimately required by many ethical theories and, already, partly embodied within many of the caring professions. *Agape* may also be used to denote the relationship of artists to their art or scientists to a natural world that spontaneously evokes awe and wonder. In this way, secular experience (which, in terms of transposition theory, may not be all that secular) is seen afresh and moulded theologically.

Negatively, this implies, again, a permanent judgment on secular structures that always fall short of *agape* in its full theological sense. It is not just situations that grossly distort *agape* (nuclear wars, genocide, environmental pollution) which fall under this judgment, but even well-meaning attempts to care for others which actually serve more the interests of self. *Agape* is perfectionist, it is never fully realizable within the secular realm, it permanently remains elusive and irreducible, and it does point to a theistic relationship beyond this realm. It is a truly relational model.

Within Christian ethics there is still considerable debate about whether or not *agape* is a sufficient Christian resource.[13] Critics of pure agapism frequently point to social issues, such as nuclear deterrence, to indicate that *agape* cannot resolve all moral dilemmas. Whether it can or not, a relational approach working within the framework of systematic theology will be unlikely to espouse pure agapism. Here *agape* is used as the most appropriate model of sanctification within present-day Western society. No claim is made that it is the only possible model to use. As a model within systematic theology it is intended to be set alongside models of creation and redemption.

V

The final test for models in systematic theology, once their individual appropriateness is established, must be their ability to function together. In this respect, systematic theology makes different demands of its models from Christian ethics. The Christian ethicist rightly focusses upon specific moral issues and brings theological, ethical and social resources to bear upon these issues. Even if the Christian ethicist is not specifically concerned with moral decision-making, it is nonetheless the moral issue itself that determines which resources are most appropriate in a particular social context. The systematic theologian, in contrast, is committed to a more ambitious theological framework. It does become a matter of central importance to know how models used in ethical areas relate to models used to denote the themes of creation and redemption. The systematic theologian harbours the belief that models from the themes of creation, redemption and sanctification can be mutually and beneficially inter-related and that theological vision is constricted and impaired if this is not done.

The adeodatic, teleological and agapistic models suggested here can be inter-related through their mutual weaknesses or combined to give a more balanced denotation of the theistic relationship upon which they are based. Some of their individual weaknesses have already been noted. In every instance it has been suggested that the other models serve to mollify them.

Givenness may sometimes appear arbitrary and may not always appear to be the fruit of a sustained and caring relationship. The teleological model responds to this sense of arbitrariness which is so strong a feature of present-day Western pluralism. The agapistic model affirms that secular discernments of givenness really are discernments of a sustained and deep relationship. Purposiveness may be fabricated and may, as a result, simply be some selfish attempt to mould the world in one's own image. It is germane to the sociology of knowledge initially to regard all labels, typologies, and forms of hermeneutics as socially relative (even within the physical sciences) and frequently as more instructive about the people using them than about the realities to which they are meant to refer. However, the adeodatic model attempts to ground purposiveness in the world of everyday experience. Without claiming that this experience itself is unambiguously teleological, it does nonetheless attempt to relate the teleology fostered through religious socialization to this experience. Thus givenness is not in itself teleological, but it does become so once related to the teleological model. The selfish tendencies of purposiveness are also countered by the agapistic model, which insists that the interests of others must be determinative. And *agape*, on its own, can appear uncontrollable and even anarchic. Its ability to elude careful definition, to attract sentimentality, and to function only with difficulty in the social realm, all contribute to its uncontrollability. Purposiveness, on the other hand, mollifies its inherent anarchism and givenness focusses it into partially attainable objectives. Neither can wholly control *agape*: it continues to witness to the outpouring of faith and of the need to sustain faith in action. Yet the models in combination avoid some of the obvious weaknesses of pure agapism.

Once these three models are seen in combination a variety of patterns emerges. Despite some claims to orthodoxy, it is now apparent to many scholars that the New Testament contains a rich variety of christological, binitarian and trinitarian models.[14] Credal formalism has tended to impose a harmonized version of these models and it has taken the work of careful redaction criticism to re-establish the riches contained in the New Testament itself. A variety of patterns becomes apparent from this scholarship, patterns which can serve as a paradigm for the various combinations possible between the models here. Sometimes two of the models can perform an adjectival role and the third the substantive role. Sometimes just two of the models can be combined. Sometimes their traditional order can be reversed and givenness can be taken last. The patterns can be varied according to the specific social contexts within which they are to be used. It is exactly this which characterizes the New Testament use of models.

The strength of adeodatic language is that it attempts to relate to secular experience and to re-interpret this experience in eminently theistic and relational terms. Life identified as God-given is endowed with value and dignity and should evoke a sense of gratitude and responsibility. Combined with the other two models the giver and the givenness are seen as purposeful and loving. Purposeful gifts instruct in a way that random gifts may not. Loving gifts reinforce a reciprocal relationship in a way that gifts of duty or, worse, competitive status, do not. Yet once our relationship to God is seen in terms of a purposeful and loving givenness, it is clear that it is God who is the initiator. Thus the relationship implies reciprocity, but it also stresses that the initiative belongs to the giver. It is the giver, too, who is purposeful and loving: the recipients are invited to respond in kind, first with gratitude and then with purpose and love themselves.

The strength of teleological language is that it responds to present-day Western pluralism and suggests the development of order through involvement in a religious tradition. The dream of Western liberalism is that order can be established intellectually without recourse to any religious tradition. The teleological model would suggest that this will remain just a dream, both because of the extent of a pluralism which can be reduced successfully only by extensive socialization (in which religious traditions have long and tested experience), and because purpose is never wholly convincing if it is known simply to be fabricated. Given and loving purpose suggests an understanding of purpose which is neither fabricated nor selfish. Purpose is properly seen as given only in this sense and not in the sense that it should be evident to all rational people, whether or not they belong to a religious tradition. In christological terms, purpose is given in Jesus Christ: in him the very purpose of God is embodied and becomes evident to others within the community that owes its existence to him.

The strength of agapistic language is that it responds to evidence of real care in Western society and seeks to re-locate its roots and the means to sustain it even within a pluralist and functionalist society. Care is now identified as *agape* and *agape* is identified as an explicitly theological model. *Agape* is concerned not just with relationships between people, but also with their relationship to God and, first and foremost, with God's relationship to the world. In theology the first two relationships are dependent upon the last. *Agape* is seen as both given and purposeful. It is given in the sense that it is God who is the prime lover: our own love of God and love of neighbours is dependent upon God as the initiator and sustainer of this love. It is purposeful also because it is willed, planned and intended by God: it is not arbitrary or fortuitous love. But it is also purposeful in the sense that it is intended for us to shape our own faith and behaviour in terms of *agape* and then to go out and shape society at large also in terms of *agape*. Finally *agape* is purposeful in an eschatological sense. *Agape* seeks to draw all things into the final purpose of the divine giver – life in God.

Notes

1. Relative Convictions

1. Peter L. Berger, *A Rumour of Angels*, Doubleday 1967 and Penguin 1969.

2. See W. S. F. Pickering, *Durkheim on Religion*, Routledge & Kegan Paul 1975, and *Durkheim's Sociology of Religion: Themes and Theories*, Routledge & Kegan Paul 1984.

3. See further my *Theology and Sociology: A Reader*, Geoffrey Chapman 1987 and Paulist Press 1988.

4. Ibid.

5. See E. Schillebeeckx, *Ministry: A Case for Change*, SCM Press 1981 and *The Church with a Human Face*, SCM Press 1985.

6. See Graham Shaw, *The Cost of Authority: Manipulation and Freedom in the New Testament*, SCM Press 1983.

2. Fundamentalist Convictions

1. See E. Sandeen, *The Roots of Fundamentalism: British and American Millenerianism 1800–1930*, University of Chicago Press 1970, p. 246; see also G. Marsden, *Fundamentalism and American Culture: The Shaping of Twentieth-Century Evangelicalism 1870–1925*, OUP 1980.

2. *The Fundamentals*, Testimony Publishing Company, Chicago 1910–15.

3. R. Hrair Dekmejian, *Islam in Revolution: Fundamentalism in the Arab World*, Syracuse University Press 1985, p. 4.

4. James Barr, *Fundamentalism*, SCM Press [2]1981.

5. See Peter. L. Berger, *Facing up to Modernity: Excursions in Society, Politics and Religion*, Penguin 1977, and *The Heretical Imperative: Contemporary Possibilities of Religious Affirmation*, Collins 1980. But see also essays in L. Caplan (ed.), *Studies in Religious Fundamentalism*, State University of New York Press 1987.

6. Introduction to E. Gellner (ed.), *Islamic Dilemmas: Reformers, Nationalists and Industrialization*, Mouton 1985, p. 6.

7. Ibid., p. 7.

8. Ibid., pp. 7–8.

9. Dekmejian, op. cit., p. 32. See also Roy Mottahedeh, *The Mantle of the Prophet: Religion and Politics in Iran*, Pantheon 1985.

10. Sami Zubaida, 'The Quest for the Islamic State: Islamic Fundamentalism in Egypt and Iran' in L. Caplan (ed.), op. cit., p 49.

11. E. Sivan, *Radical Islam: Medieval Theology and Modern Politics*, Yale University Press 1985, p. 188.

12. See Roger Ruston, 'Apocalyptic and the Peace Movement', *New Blackfriars* 67, 791, May 1986.

13. Ian S. Lustick, *For the Land and the Lord: Jewish Fundamentalism in Israel*, Council on Foreign Relations, NY 1988, p. 44. For the effect of the 1967 War on Egyptian Sunni fundamentalists, see Sivan, op. cit.

14. Lustick, op. cit., p. 9.

15. Ibid., pp. 177–8.

16. Ibid., p. 5.

17. Ibid., p. 6.

18. See L. Caplan, 'Fundamentalism as Counter-Culture' in Caplan (ed.), op. cit.

19. Barr, op. cit. See also Richard Tapper and Nancy Tapper, '"Thank God We're Secular!" Aspects of Fundamentalism in a Turkish Town', in Caplan (ed.) op. cit.

20. Cf. Berger, 1977 and 1980, op. cit.

21. E.g. Introduction to Caplan (ed.), op. cit., pp. 14–15.

22. See A. Walker, 'Fundamentalism and Modernity: The Restoration Movement in Britain', in Caplan (ed.), op. cit.

23. Dekmejian, op. cit. pp. 7–8.

24. An exception that Dekmejian cites is Bernard Lewis, 'The Return of Islam', *Commentary*, 61 (Jan. 1976), pp. 39–49: others have cited predictions published later in Michael M. J. Fischer's *Iran: From Religious Dispute to Revolution*, Harvard University Press 1980, and Hamid Algar's *The Roots of the Islamic Revolution*, Open Press, The Muslim Institute, 1983.

25. See R. Gill, *The Social Context of Theology*, Mowbrays 1975 and *Prophecy and Praxis*, Marshall, Morgan & Scott 1981.

26. Bryan Wilson, *Religion in Secular Society*, Watts 1966, and *Contemporary Transformations of Religion*, OUP 1976.

27. Peter L. Berger, *The Sacred Canopy*, Doubleday 1967: British title, *The Social Reality of Religion*, Faber 1969.

28. S. S. Acquaviva, *The Decline of the Sacred in Industrial Society*, 1966, trs P. Lipscomb, Harper & Row 1979.

29. Ibid., p. 48.

30. Ibid., p. 85.

31. Ibid., p. 35.

32. Ibid., pp. 200–2.

33. E.g. see P. E. Glasner, *The Sociology of Secularisation*, Routledge & Kegan Paul 1977.

34. See Sivan, op. cit., p. 183.

35. J. Obelkevich, L. Roper and R. Samuel (eds), *Disciplines of Faith: Studies in Religion, Politics and Patriarchy*, Routledge & Kegan Paul 1987.

36. Ibid., pp. 5–6.

37. See further, chapter 4.

38. S. D. Johnson and J. B. Tamney (eds), *The Political Role of Religion in the United States*, Westview Press 1986.

39. Ibid., p. 1.

40. Ibid., p. 3.

41. Phillip E. Hammond (ed.), *The Sacred in a Secular Age*, University of California Press 1984: see also James A. Beckford and Thomas Luckmann (eds), *The Changing Face of Religion*, Sage 1989.

42. See P. H. Vrijhof and J. Waardenburg, *Official and Popular Religion: Analysis of a Theme for Religious Studies*, Mouton 1979.

43. S. M. Bhardwaj and G. Rinschede (eds), *Pilgrimage in World Reli-*

gions: Geographia Religionum, Interdisziplinare Schriftenreihe zur Religions-geographie, Band 4, Dietrich Reimer Verlag 1988, p. 11.

44. See Alistair Kee, *Domination or Liberation: The Place of Religion in Social Conflict*, SCM Press 1986, ch. 4.

45. Harvey Cox, *Religion in the Secular City: Toward a Postmodern Theology*, Simon & Schuster 1984.

46. Harvey Cox, *The Secular City: Urbanization and Secularization in Theological Perspective*, Macmillan and SCM Press 1965.

47. See R. Gill, op. cit., 1975.

48. See Harvey Cox, *The Silencing of Leonardo Boff*, Meyer Stone 1988.

49. Cox, *Religion in the Secular City*, p. 50.

50. Ibid., p. 74.

51. L. Caplan, *Class and Culture in Urban India: Fundamentalism in a Christian Community*, OUP 1987, p. 254.

52. See J. K. Hadden and C. E. Swann, *Prime-time Preachers: the Rising Power of Televangelism*, Addison-Wesley 1981: see also Steve Bruce, *The Rise and Fall of the New Christian Right: Conservative Protestant Politics in America 1978–88*, OUP 1988.

53. See Dekmejian, op. cit., and Ali E. Hillal Dessouki (ed.), *Islamic Resurgence in the Arab World*, Praeger 1982.

54. Steve Bruce, 'The Moral Majority: the Politics of Fundamentalism in Secular Society', in Capan (ed.), op. cit., p. 191.

3. Impending Convictions

1. See Roger Ruston, 'Apocalyptic and the Peace Movement', *New Black-friars* 67, p. 791, May 1986.

2. See n. 24 of ch. 2.

3. Leon Festinger, Henry W. Riecken and Stanley Schachter, *When Prophecy Fails: A Social and Psychological Study of a Modern Group that Predicted the Destruction of the World*, Harper Torchbooks 1956.

4. Ibid., p. 3.

5. Ibid., p. 4.

6. Ibid., pp. 30–1.

7. Leon Festinger, *A Theory of Cognitive Dissonance*, Evanston 1957.

8. See further, essays in Norman K. Gottwald (ed.) *The Bible and Liberation: Political and Social Hermeneutics*, Orbis 1983, and Robin Gill (ed.) *Theology and Sociology: a Reader*, Geoffrey Chapman 1987 and Paulist Press 1988.

9. Robert P. Carroll, *When Prophecy Failed: Reactions and Responses to Failure in the Old Testament Prophectic Tradition*, SCM Press 1979.

10. Ibid., p. 215.

11. Robert P. Carroll, 'Ancient Israelite Prophecy and Dissonance Theory', *Numen*, XXIV, 2, 1977, p. 148.

12. John G. Gager, *Kingdom and Community: the Social World of Early Christianity*, Prentice Hall 1975.

13. Especially Wayne A. Meeks, *The First Urban Christians: the Social World of the Apostle Paul*, Yale University Press 1983.

14. Especially Norman K. Gottwald, *The Tribes of Yahweh: a Sociology of the Religion of Liberated Israel, 1250–1050 B.C.E.*, Orbis Books and SCM Press 1979 and *The Hebrew Bible: A Socio-Literary Introduction*. Fortress 1985.

15. Gager, p. 11.

16. Ibid., p. 2.

17. E.g. J. A. Hardyck and Braden, 'Prophecy Fails Again: a Report of a Failure to Replicate', *Journal of Abnormal and Social Psychology*, 65, 1962.

18. See further, Gottwald (ed.) and Gill (ed.), op. cit.

19. E.g. Ian Hamnett, 'Sociology of Religion and Sociology of Error', *Religion*, 3, 1973: although see his 'A Mistake about Error', *New Blackfriars* 67, 788, Feb. 1986.

20. See Hans H. Penner, 'Rationality and Religion: Problems in the Comparison of Modes of Thought', *Journal of the American Academy of Religion* LIV, 4, 1987.

21. See Gottwald (ed.), op. cit.

22. See Bryan Wilson, *Religion in Sociological Perspective*, OUP 1982.

23. *When Prophecy Fails*, p. 249.

24. Alison Lurie, *Imaginary Friends*, Heinemann 1967 and Abacus 1987.

25. Ibid., pp. 4–5.

26. *When Prophecy Fails*, p. 165.

27. Ibid., p. vi.

28. Bruce J. Malina, 'Normative Dissonance and Christian Origins', *Semeia*, 35, 1986, p. 39.

4. *Understanding Church Decline*

1. See Bryan S. Turner, 'The Sociological Explanation of Ecumenicalism', in C. L. Mitton (ed.), *The Social Sciences and the Churches*, T. & T. Clark 1972.

2. Rodney Stark and William Sims Bainbridge, *The Future of Religion: Secularization, Revival, and Cult Formation*, University of California Press 1985.

3. H. Richard Niebuhr, *The Social Sources of Denominationalism*, Henry Holt 1929.

4. Christine King, 'The Case of the Third Reich', in Eileen Barker (ed.) *New Religious Movements: A Perspective for Understanding Society*, Edwin Mellen 1982.

5. Ibid., p. 130.

6. Ibid., pp. 134–5.

7. Bryan Wilson, *Contemporary Transformations of Religion: The Riddell Memorial Lectures, Forty-fifth Series, delivered at the University of Newcastle upon Tyne on 2, 3, 4 December 1974*, OUP 1976.

8. Ibid., p. vii.

9. Ibid., p. 6.

10. Ibid., p. 13.

11. Ibid., p. 27.

12. Ibid., pp. 14–15.

13. Ibid., p. 22.

14. See Bryan Wilson, *Religion in Sociological Perspective*, OUP 1982, ch. 6; Wilson in Phillip Hammond (eds.), *The Sacred in a Secular Age*, University of California Press 1984; Wilson in Stewart Sutherland (ed.), *The World's Religions*, Routledge & Kegan Paul 1988; and Wilson 'The Functions of Religion: A Reappraisal', *Religion*, 1988, 18, pp. 199–216.

15. Wilson, *Religion in Sociological Perspective*, p. 110.

16. Wilson, *Contemporary Transformations*, pp. 23–4.

17. Hammond, *The Sacred in a Secular Age*, p. 2.

18. J. Obelkevich, L. Roper and R. Samuel (eds), *Disciplines of Faith: Studies in Religion, Politics and Patriarchy*, Routledge & Kegan Paul 1987.

19. Ibid., p.6.

20. See Stephen Yeo, *Religion and Voluntary Organisations in Crisis*, Croom Helm 1976; James Obelkevich, *Religion and Rural Society: South Lindsey 1825–1875*, OUP 1976; Jeffrey Cox, *The English Churches in a Secular Society: Lambeth, 1870–1930*, OUP 1982; Callum Brown, *The Social History of Religion in Scotland since 1730*, Methuen 1987.

21. J. Cox, op. cit., p. 265.

22. Ibid., p. 266.

23. See David Martin, *The Religious and the Secular*, Routledge & Kegan Paul 1969.

24. J. Cox, op. cit., p. 273.

25. Priscilla J. Brewer, *Shaker Communities, Shaker Lives*, University Press of New England 1986.

26. Obelkevich, *Religion and Rural Society*, op. cit.

27. Horace Mann, *1851 Census Great Britain: Report and Tables on Religious Worship England and Wales*, British Parliamentary Papers, Population 10, 1852–3, p. cxxi (reprinted by Irish University Press 1970).

28. See Alan Everitt, *The Pattern of Rural Dissent: the Nineteenth Century*, Leicester University Press 1972.

29. J. Cox, op. cit. p. 276.

30. For these effects see Leslie Francis, *Rural Anglicanism*, Collins 1985.

31. See further my *Beyond Decline*, SCM Press 1988.

32. See Stephen Sykes, *The Identity of Christianity*, SPCK 1984; and D. Hardy and D. Ford, *Jubilate*, Darton, Longman & Todd 1985.

5. *Competing Convictions and Declining Churches*

1. See Table 7.

2. See Bryan S. Turner, 'The Sociological Explanation of Ecumenicalism', in C. L. Mitton (ed.), *The Social Sciences and the Churches*, T. & T. Clark 1972.

3. See Robert Currie, *Methodism Divided*, Faber 1968.

4. See David M. Thompson, 'Church Extension in Town and Countryside in Late Nineteenth-Century Leicestershire', in Derek Baker (ed.), *The Church in Town and Countryside: Studies in Church History, Vol 15*, Blackwell 1979, pp. 427–440.

5. Robert Currie, Alan Gilbert and Lee Horsley, *Churches and Church-goers*, CUP 1977: a weakness of Kevin J. Christiano's *Religious Diversity and Social Change: American Cities, 1890–1906*, CUP 1987, is that it relies heavily upon the poorest of all indicators, namely religious affiliation.

6. *Clergy Visitation Returns 1810 Vol III*, Auckland Castle Episcopal Records, held in the Department of Palaeography and Diplomatic, University of Durham.

7. Ibid., p. 316.

8. Ibid., p. 200.

9. Ibid., p. 347.

10. Ibid., p. 262.

11. *Clergy Visitation Returns 1861*, Auckland Castle Episcopal Records, held in the Department of Palaeography and Diplomatic, University of

Durham (these Returns to the Bishop should not be confused with the separate
Returns to the Archdeacon, which were made in the same years but are more
concerned with the state of repair of the various parish buildings).

12. Ibid.

13. Ibid.

14. Ibid.

15. Ibid.

16. *Clergy Visitation Returns 1866*, Auckland Castle Episcopal Records,
held in the Department of Palaeography and Diplomatic, University of
Durham.

17. Ibid.

18. Ibid.

19. *Clergy Visitation Returns 1870*, Auckland Castle Episcopal Records,
held in the Department of Palaeography and Diplomatic, University of
Durham.

20. Ibid.

21. Ibid.

22. *Clergy Visitation Returns 1874*, Auckland Castle Episcopal Records,
held in the Department of Palaeography and Diplomatic, University of
Durham.

23. Ibid.

24. Ibid.

25. Ibid.

26. For the 1880s see *Clergy Visitation Returns 1887*, Diocese of Newcastle,
held in Northumberland Record Office, Gosforth.

27. *Clergy Visitation Returns 1866*, Auckland Castle Episcopal Records,
held in the Department of Palaeography and Diplomatic, University of
Durham.

28. *Clergy Visitation Returns 1891*, Diocese of Newcastle, held in Northumberland Record Office, Gosforth.

29. Ibid.

30. Ibid.

31. Ibid.

32. Ibid.

33. *Clergy Visitation Returns 1899*, Diocese of Newcastle, held in Northumberland Record Office, Gosforth.

34. Ibid.

35. Ibid.

36. Ibid.

37. Ibid.

38. Ibid.

39. *Clergy Visitation Returns 1903*, Diocese of Newcastle, held in Northumberland Record Office, Gosforth.

40. *Minutes of the Presbytery of Berwick, Vol. I*, held in Northumberland
Record Office, Gosforth.

41. Ibid.

42. Still held by Crookham United Reformed Church.

43. George M'Guffie, *The Priests of Etal: or Annals of Tillside*, Darien Press,
Edinburgh, 1890s, various editions.

44. Hastings M. Neville, *Under a Border Tower*, Mawson, Swan & Morgan,
Newcastle upon Tyne 1897.

45. M'Guffie, op. cit., 4th edition p. 6.

46. Held in Northumberland Record Office, Gosforth.

47. *Clergy Visitation Returns 1874*, Auckland Castle Episcopal Records, held in the Department of Palaeography and Diplomatic, University of Durham.

48. Minutes still held by Crookham United Reformed Church.

49. Minutes still held by Crookham United Reformed Church.

50. *Minutes of the Presbytery of Berwick, Vol. I*, held in Northumberland Record Office, Gosforth.

51. Ibid.

52. All Communion Rolls still held by Crookham United Reformed Church.

53. According to the return for the 1851 Religious Census.

54. See J. Mackie, 'Branton Congregation, Northumberland: Three Documents, 1772–1856', *Journal of the Presbyterian Historical Society*, 1, XIII, 1964.

55. Minutes still held by Crookham United Reformed Church.

56. Beaumont Church Communion Rolls for 1937–74 held in Northumberland Record Office, Gosforth.

57. Lowick Scotch Church Communion Rolls from 1848 held in Northumberland Record Office, Gosforth.

58. Estimate from an MS of the 1880s by John Black, held in Northumberland Record Office, Gosforth.

59. Report held in Northumberland Record Office, Gosforth.

60. Estimate from an MS of the 1880s by John Black, held in Northumberland Record Office, Gosforth.

61. Report held in Northumberland Record Office, Gosforth.

62. *Clergy Visitation Returns 1810 Vol. III and 1814*, Auckland Castle Episcopal Records, held in the Department of Palaeography and Diplomatic, University of Durham.

63. Summary only of *Clergy Visitation Returns 1857*, Auckland Castle Episcopal Records, held in the Department of Palaeography and Diplomatic, University of Durham.

64. *Clergy Visitation Returns 1887*, Diocese of Newcastle, held in Northumberland Record Office, Gosforth.

65. *Clergy Returns 1986*, held in Church House, London.

66. See J. Mackie, 'Branton Congregation, Northumberland: Three Documents, 1772–1856', *Journal of the Presbyterian Historical Society*, 1, XIII, 1964.

67. The Communion Roll of Chatton Church for 1850–1853 suggests that 46 of its members were transferred from Cheviot Street Presbyterian Church in Wooler and 17 from Tower Hill: held in Church House, Tavistock Place, London.

68. The earliest Communion Rolls for Beaumont Church have apparently not survived: those for 1901–1936 are held at Church House, Tavistock Place, London, and those for 1937–1974 at Northumberland Record Office, Gosforth.

69. Copy of sermon held in Northumberland Record Office, Gosforth.

70. Copy of pastoral letter held in Northumberland Record Office, Gosforth.

71. Copy of pastoral letter held in Northumberland Record Office, Gosforth.

72. Letter held in Northumberland Record Office, Gosforth.

73. Appeal notice held in Northumberland Record Office, Gosforth.

74. Letter held in Northumberland Record Office, Gosforth.

75. All Catholic statistics are taken from *Status Animarum*, held in North-umberland Record Office, Gosforth.

76. All Primitive Methodist statistics are taken from *Lowick Circuit Minutes*, held in Northumberland Record Office, Gosforth.

77. See J. N. Wolfe and M. Pickford, *The Church of Scotland: An Economic Survey*, Chapman 1980.

78. See Leslie J. Francis, *Rural Anglicanism*, Collins 1985.

6. The Effects of Competing Convictions

1. See Horace Mann's *Report* in the *1851 Census Great Britain: Report and Tables on Religious Worship: England and Wales*. British Parliamentary Papers, 10, 1852–3, pp. cxixf.

2. James Obelkevich, *Religion and Rural Society: South Lindsey 1825–1875*, OUP 1976.

3. See David Martin, *The Religious and the Secular*, Routledge & Kegan Paul 1969; 'The Secularization Question', *Theology*, LXXVI, 630, 1973; and *A General Theory of Secularization*, Blackwell 1978.

4. See Larry Shiner, 'The Meanings of Secularisation', *International Year-book for the Sociology of Religion*, III, 1967, reprinted in James F. Childress and David B. Harned (eds). *Secularisation and the Protestant Prospect*, West-minster 1970.

5. Obelkevich, op. cit. p. 324.

6. Ibid. p. 324.

7. Ibid., pp. 324–5.

8. Ibid., pp. 325–6.

9. See Mann, op. cit.

10. Calculated by dividing 1851 seating by 1901 total population × 100.

11. Calculated by dividing 1851 seating by 1971 total population × 100.

12. Calculated by dividing 1851 seating by the same percentage of the 1901 total population as attended church for each service time per denomination in 1851 × 100.

13. As they existed in 1851: there were of course slight changes by 1901, losing a few rural districts and adding urban ones.

14. I am most grateful to Miss Sheila Smith for this research, in rural parishes around Hexham and Haydon Bridge.

15. For a discussion of the Index Value related to the 1851 Religious Census see: K. S. Inglis, 'Patterns of Religious Worship in 1851', *Journal of Ecclesiastical History*, 11, 1, 1960, p. 74–86; R. B. Walker, 'Religious Changes in Cheshire, 1750–1850', *Journal of Ecclesiastical History*, 17, 1, 1966, pp. 77–94; R. B. Walker, 'Religious Changes in Liverpool in the Nineteenth Century', *Journal of Ecclesiastical History*, 19. 2, 1968, pp. 195–211;.D. M. Thompson, 'The 1851 Religious Census: Problems and Possibilities', *Victorian Studies*, 11, 1967, pp. 87–97.

16. Callum Brown documents this well in 'Did Urbanisation Secularise Britain?', *Urban History Yearbook*, 1988: see also his *The Social History of Religion in Scotland Since 1730*, Methuen 1987, ch. 5.

17. Ibid., 1988, p. 17.

18. Ibid., p. 18.

19. See *Faith in the City*, The Report of the Archbishop of Canterbury's Commission on Urban Priority Areas, Church House Publishing 1985.

20. See chapter 4; see also W. C. Roof and W. McKinney, *American Mainline Religion*, Rutgers 1987.

21. See Jeffrey Cox, *The English Churches in a Secular Society: Lambeth, 1870–1930*, OUP 1982.

22. See Callum Brown, op. cit.

23. Ibid.

24. See Hugh Macleod, 'Class, Community and Region: The Religious Geography of Nineteenth-Century England', in Michael Hill (ed.), *Sociological Yearbook of Religion in Britain*, 6, SCM Press 1973, pp. 29–72.

25. Nigel Yates, 'Urban Church Attendance and the Use of Statistical Evidence, 1850–1900', in Derek Baker (ed.), *The Church in Town and Countryside*, Vol. 16, Blackwell 1979, p. 392.

26. See Cox, op. cit.

27. See Andrew Mearns, *The Statistics of Attendance at Public Worship: As Published in England, Wales and Scotland by the Local Press, Between October 1881 and February 1882*, Hodder 1882 (a copy is in the Bodleian Library, Oxford). Newcastle counted morning and estimated other attendances.

28. See Jane T. Stoddart, 'The Daily News Census of 1902–3 Compared with the British Weekly Census of 1886', in Richard Mudie-Smith (ed.), *The Religious Life of London*, Hodder 1904, for evidence of central London Church of England churches showing similar aggregate reductions.

29. E. R. Wickham, *Church and People in an Industrial Society*, Lutterworth Press 1957.

30. See Michael P. Hornsby-Smith, *Roman Catholics in England*, CUP 1987.

31. See Callum Brown's calculations based upon the 1979–84 Bible Society census, 'Religion', in Rex Pope (ed.), *Atlas of British Social and Economic History*, Routledge & Kegan Paul 1989, pp. 211–223.

32. Hornsby-Smith, op. cit., p. 211.

33. Changes in London churchgoing can be calculated from comparing the 1851 Religious Census results with those reported in the British Weekly's *The Religious Census of London*, Hodder 1888, and those in Mudie-Smith 1904, op. cit.

7. Relativism in Modern Theology

1. E. Schillebeeckx, *Ministry: A Case for Change*, SCM Press 1981.

2. SCM Press 1985.

3. *Ministry*, p. 39.

4. Ibid., p. 66.

5. Ibid., p. 56.

6. Gregory Baum, *Religion and Alienation: A Theological Reading of Sociology*, Paulist Press 1975.

7. *Ministry*, p. 57.

8. Ibid., p. 155.

9. See further my *Theology and Sociology: A Reader*, Geoffrey Chapman 1987 and Paulist Press 1988.

10. See further my *A Textbook of Christian Ethics*, T. & T. Clark 1985.

11. *On Idolatry*, 19, *The Ante-Nicene Fathers*, 3, Eerdmans/T. & T. Clark.

12. *Reply to Faustus the Manichaean*, XXII.69, *The Nicene and Post-Nicene Fathers*, 4, Eerdmans/T. & T. Clark.

13. *Summa Theologica*, 2a2ae, 40.2, Vol 35, Blackfriars with Eyre & Spottiswoode 1972.

14. In *Theology and Sociology*, op. cit.

15. Yale 1983.

16. Prentice-Hall 1975.

17. Wayne A. Meeks, 'The Man from Heaven in Johannine Sectarianism', *Journal of Biblical Studies*, 91, 1972.

18. A position made explicit in Robert A. Oden Jr, *The Bible Without Theology*, Harper & Row 1987.

19. Graham Shaw, *The Cost of Authority*, SCM Press 1983, p. vii.

20. Stephen Sykes, *The Identity of Christianity*, SPCK 1984, pp. 51–2.

21. Ibid., pp. 76–7.

22. Stephen Sykes, *The Integrity of Anglicanism*, Mowbrays 1978.

23. Ibid., p. 276.

24. Ibid., pp. 282–3.

8. *Theology – A Social System*

1. See Karl Mannheim, *Ideology and Utopia*, Routledge & Kegan Paul 1936.

2. Peter McKenzie, *The Christians: Their Practices and Beliefs*, SPCK 1988, provides a very useful phenomenological account of the diversity of Christianity in the modern world.

3. See further my *Theology and Sociology: A Reader*, Geoffrey Chapman 1987 and Paulist Press 1988.

4. See Max Black, *Models and Metaphors*, Cornell University Press 1962.

5. See Ian G. Barbour, *Issues in Science and Religion*, SCM Press 1966: and more recently, John Polkinghorne, *Science and Creation: The Search for Understanding*, SPCK 1988.

6. See Aquinas, *Summa Theologica*, 1a2ae, 96, 4f.

7. See Peter L. Berger, *The Heretical Imperative: Contemporary Possibilities of Religious Affirmation*, Collins 1980: and, with Brigitte Berger and Hansfried Kellner, *The Homeless Mind: Modernization and Consciousness*, Penguin 1973.

8. See F. G. Bailey (ed.), *Gifts and Poison: The Politics of Reputation*, Blackwell 1971.

9. See Richard M. Titmuss, *The Gift Relationship*, Penguin 1973.

10. E.g. Rodney Stark and William Sims Bainbridge, *The Future of Religion: Secularization, Revival, and Cult Formation*, University of California Press 1985.

11. See Paul Badham in *Expository Times*, 97, 10, July 1986.

12. See Paul Avis, *Ecumenical Theology*, SPCK 1986 and my own *Beyond Decline*, SCM Press 1988.

13. See further my *A Textbook of Christian Ethics*, T. & T. Clark 1985.

14. See James P. Mackey, *The Christian Experience of God as Trinity*, SCM Press 1983; and James D. G. Dunn and James P. Mackey, *New Testament Theology in Dialogue*, SPCK 1987.

Index